TOUGH AND TENDER

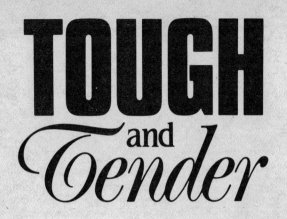

TOUGH and *Tender*

JOYCE LANDORF

KINGSWAY PUBLICATIONS
EASTBOURNE

Copyright © Fleming H. Revell Co. 1975, 1981

First published in the USA by Fleming H. Revell Co.,
Old Tappan, New Jersey

First British edition 1983

ISBN 0 86065 264 5

Printed in Great Britain for
KINGSWAY PUBLICATIONS LTD
Lottbridge Drove, Eastbourne, E. Sussex BN23 6NT by
Richard Clay (The Chaucer Press) Ltd,
Bungay, Suffolk

Wherever he is—there is

    a newly waxed car
    a kept-up yard
    an unplugged drain
    a TV turned on to any sports event
    a motorcycle
    the refreshing scent of his after-shave
    the vanilla ice cream he makes—just so
    delicious pancakes for Saturday's breakfast
    a "right" way to do something
    a "good-morning" hug and
    a game of dominoes to be played.

Wherever he is—there are

    his strong arms
    his sure, firm steps
    games at dinnertime
    teasing and laughter in bed
    stubborn strengths
    sensitive decisions and
    gentle courtesies.

Wherever he is—there is

    praying together
    lovemaking
    great tenderness and
    all the warmth and love
    this woman could ever know.

My thanks to Brenda Arnold
and Sheila Rapp—again, and
again, and again.

Contents

TOUGH AND TENDER

1

Thanks, Wife, I Needed That!

I would have you learn this great fact: that a life of doing right is the wisest life there is. If you live that kind of life, you'll not limp or stumble as you run. Carry out my instructions; don't forget them, for they will lead you to real living.

PROVERBS 4:11–13

It's hard for me, as I look up from this printed page, to tell *exactly* what you're thinking. I can see that some of you are genuinely interested and more than a little curious as to what a woman *really* wants in her man. Heaven knows you've spent years trying to be a well-balanced husband and you've done a pretty good job, but every once in a while you've been known to throw your hands up in the air and desperately shout, "I'm never going to understand women!"

As I look closer, however, I can see the expression on many of your faces is not some mildly curious twinkle in your eyes. You are not chuckling with, "Well, well now, what do we have here?" Actually, on some of your faces I definitely see the look of resigned disappointment. This book was not what you had envisioned at all, and the look above your eyebrows, around your eyes, and down by your mouth is clearly puzzlement, fused with a hint of frustration.

The source of your expression lies in the fact that today is not your birthday, Christmas, or Father's Day, but for days now *she* has been fluttering around your house with all the clucking and goings-on of a mother hen about to spring a great announcement. Even her walk says, "I know something you don't know."

13

A kind of *happening* has been going on with her for days. This morning you were sure of it because she *hummed* a little tune when she handed you your cold cereal for breakfast.

When you asked about the mainspring of her giddy joy and singing, you *had* hoped you'd hear your name. Instead she just hummed another line and, as she was flitting out the kitchen door, she paused long enough to wave at you and say, "Boy, have I got a surprise for you!"

"A surprise?" you thought. "Ah ha! I'll bet I know what it is! For months now she's been reading all those women's books on the how-to's of really being a fulfilled woman and a sexy wife, and now it's all going to pay off. She's going to *show* me what she's learned (she's even taken classes). This is great. I wonder what she'll do?" Delicious anticipation has scampered across your mind.

You left the house in a rather happy daze and all morning you had a delightful time fantasizing how the surprise would be handled. You hadn't read any of the books, but from what you had picked up between her friends' conversations and your daughter's remarks, you put this fantasy into motion.

You conjured up the sound of her voice calling you at the office around 10:30 A.M. asking you in a sexy way to come home for lunch. You could see it all happening in your mind's eye. Yes, you'd open the front door and there she'd be—dressed up in nothing but a frilly, see-through-net apron—and you two would have a picnic under the dining-room table. What a lunch you'd have!

However, the rumbling of your stomach brought you back to reality today because, when you looked at your watch, it was 2:30 P.M. Lunch was long gone and she hadn't called. You filed the thought, "Well, so much for the fantasy."

The drive home tonight was no different from any other night. Yet as you drove in the garage she didn't come out to meet you, and the house seemed strangely quiet. Hope gently kissed the edges of your mind, and started the fantasy going again, so you softly called, "Hon, I'm home."

After you'd wandered through the house, you found her in one of the kids' bedrooms, knee-deep in trash, holding a broken vacuum-cleaner hose in one hand and the cat in the other. She heard your "Hi!" and explained that, at the same time the vacuum cleaner broke, the cat pounced into a trash bag because he thought there was a small brown mouse trapped in there. The mess was incredible, and she wound up by saying, "Boy, am I glad you're home—you wouldn't *believe* this whole day!"

Somewhere in the back of your head the door of hope was slammed shut. You stood there looking like somebody had just rained on your parade.

Without looking up at you, she offered, "We'll have dinner as soon as I get some of this mess straightened up."

You stood there for a second or two and then said, in what can only be described as a little-boy tone, "But I thought you said this morning you had a surprise for me."

"Oh, *that.*" She picked up the cat and what was left of the trash, swept past you, and they both purred, "I do, I do, but not until *after* dinner."

Ah, hope again. This time the door of hope was not only opened, it was held open by a definitely sexy statement. Instantly you felt better!

Dinner was pretty good; the kids were in a fairly jolly mood, and your wife looked like she always looks—except for a small, but noticeable, glint around the edges of her eyes. You helped her clear off some dishes (it was the least you could do) and then settled down on the couch behind the sports page to await the moment of truth.

Finally it was time. The kitchen work was finished, the little people were put to bed, the teenager was studying to unbelievably loud music in his room, and finally your wife snuggled up from underneath your sports section and said, "Honey, *here.* This is my surprise for you."

After a whole day of running the emotional gamut from

high fantasy to low depression, you couldn't believe it!
You mumbled, "Oh, great. Fantastic. Just what I wanted."

It was a book. A book by a woman. A book about what
a woman wants in a man, and it's called *Tough and Tender.* While you looked thrilled, you were thinking,
"Thanks, wife, I needed that!"

While she sat there she kept jabbering about how some-
thing-or-other the author was—how really neat this book
was. You just kept whiling away the time by thinking, "Is
she kidding? I don't have time to keep up with all the
boring reports I have to read for my work, and now my
schooling. I've barely time to skim the sports page each
night to check out scores and standings and to take a quick
look at the financial page to review the Dow Jones. Furthermore, it's not a book about how to improve my golf
stroke, or what the football statistics are for the last
twenty years. It's a book on what *she* wants in me!"

If I have just described you and your feelings, I can
understand exactly why you are so disappointed. But, at
least for her sake, try a few pages.

This morning you were right, you know, about all those
books she's been reading lately. They've been a tremendous help to her in so many areas. She really has been
reading, studying, and discussing with others how to be
the woman, the wife, the mother, and especially the person God wants her to be. But as she's been reading those
books she has been smart enough to figure something out
for herself.

She has just begun to realize that if she desires to
change and let God really work in her own life, and her
husband is not willing to encourage, sponsor, or support
her—she's got a problem. If she has accepted God's forgiveness in her own life, and is in turn able to forgive and
accept others and the circumstances of her world, but her
husband cannot—then she has a large, unnumbered
Excedrin headache.

She feels totally alone in the struggle of day-to-day living as a wife. In fact, she feels more like a widow or a divorcée. She feels frustrated as a mother because sometimes it's as if she is raising, training, and disciplining the children with all of the problems of a *single parent*. She dreams for her marriage with you to be a real partnership. She doesn't really believe the romantic notion that marriage involves a fairy princess and a strong, brave knight riding off on his white horse into the sunset to live happily ever after. She wants a real, live marriage where two people will honor and prefer each other. She longs deeply inside her heart of hearts (and this may surprise you) for you and her to become lovers. In her reading she has read that God, the greatest author, has designed marriage to mean the leaving of parents, the cleaving to each other, and the two becoming one. She dreams of having a special love with you, a real love that does not pale and fade with years; a love that blooms, blossoms, and matures; a love that ripples and sparkles across a crowded room even after thirty years, and excludes all others as if they weren't even there.

She dearly wants all of this with you, but without your help, your encouragement, and your backing, she's bucking fantastic odds. The odds, I might add, are all *against* your marriage, your family, and your real purposes in life succeeding today, or even getting off the ground.

Anyway, dear man, I've said all of the above to really say I hope you're not *too* disappointed in this *surprise* book and that as you read it you will—

Fall madly and passionately in love with your wife.
See your children as the priceless gifts of God they really are.
Celebrate life, not mere existence. With tremendous joy and confidence *celebrate daily as the man God wants you to be.*

2

The Man or the Myth?

Let everyone be sure that he is doing his very best, for then he will have the personal satisfaction of work well done, and won't need to compare himself with someone else.

GALATIANS 6:4

The dictionary defines the word *man* as, "an adult male person," but the definition hardly scratches the surface of *what* a man truly is, or what we even *think* a man is all about when we try to describe him.

The definition leaves us standing idly in large, empty rooms with no ideas relating to what a man really is. We cannot list the true traits of a man's character. We have little or no knowledge of his inner strengths, or what makes him happy or hostile. We are barely aware of what limits him or handicaps him. Saddest of all is the emerging fact that we know precious little about the goings-on in his inner soul. The smallest ticking of his heart cannot be heard by most of us because our ears have been closed by the voices of others' opinions and measurements. We are blind to a man's spiritual feelings and his questing for faith because he hides them well in some vague, gray zone deep within him. In short, when we meet a man we are left on our own to imagine or fantasize the true measure of him, and the real meaning of this man escapes us.

The man, in one area of our life, has a significant meaning. For instance, to the police officer in a patrol car, the radio call of "See the man" means a citizen is in trouble, has a problem, or needs assistance. The instructions of "See the man" are followed by a code number which tells the officer what type of situation he will encounter. On

the other side of law enforcement, however, is the law-
breaker to whom the term "See the man" is the best
reason for yelling to his buddies, "Let's get out of here!"
The man to him means anyone (police, judge, or head
honcho) in authority.

What interests me about the term "see the man" is the
reasoning that, while I'm not a police officer or a criminal,
every day *I see the man* in our society, and yet what have
I seen when I've looked at him? Did I merely glance,
gaze, and scan; or did I contemplate, regard, and observe?
Have I seen only the dictionary's "adult male person" and
missed most of the man? Did I really see anything of the
true measure of the man? Probably not. At least I've not
seen him in the light of his potential, but rather by his
shadows, and they are illusive and vague.

Many of our ideas and concepts about men have been
subtly and skillfully shaped by Madison Avenue advertis-
ing which bombards us daily in every media possible. It
is most difficult to separate the media-myth man from the
genuine, highly original man whom God so skillfully
created. Sometimes we get so used to seeing the man's
shadows we forget what his face and soul are all about.

A full-page ad was run in the *Los Angeles Times* (Tues-
day, November 26, 1974) to statistically prove that more
men read *Playboy* than see the Monday night football
game on TV. After the copy presented the facts backing
up their claim, they ended their carefully structured
words with the sentence, "That's why *Playboy* is in a class
by itself when it comes to influencing men."

The business of influencing men is very serious. Much
money rides on it, and *Playboy* wasn't just expressing a
vague wish or hope—they *are* very influential in setting
concepts and ideals for men. Later in this chapter I want
to take a look at these standards and goals and try to
separate fact from fiction.

Not only *Playboy* magazine, but all forms of media tell
us when a man is supposed to be on the ladder of success,

what he is expected to do, and especially how he's to look while he's doing it. Each year this all adds up to a highly stylized mythical conception about men. Billions of dollars perpetuate what I believe are unreal and false standards for the majority of men today.

Subconsciously, without our awareness, we begin to accept and take on the looks of these images and concepts as if they were *truth* and *fact* when actually they are neither. They are myths, connected like a string of pearls and clasped tightly by a highly motivated group of image-setters. The string of precious pearls they dangle are picture-perfect, *but they hang just outside of most men's grasps.*

Last night nine out of ten commercials aired on TV relating to domestic products were practically documentaries on the man who *knows* which dog food to buy, what unplugs a clogged drain, and which mouthwash is twice as strong. I cringed down into the couch as I watched because, if I use my head at all, I know that in real life the average man of the house *rarely* has time to feed the dog, is *never* at home when the drain stops up, and hardly ever *goes* to the supermarket or drugstore to buy mouthwash —much less knows which one. But ever upward and onward goes the myth.

I think what irritates me the most is that, even though I know about the myths, I fall right smack into their elaborate trap when I'm asked to describe a man. I tell how he looks, what he eats or drinks, where he goes for pleasure, how hard he works and at what, how he dresses, what kind of car he drives, and if his insurance is in good hands or not. Without realizing it I'm repeating the commercials, and they have hooked me!

As if it weren't enough with television commercials popping out at us like cuckoo birds from a clock every 12 1/2 minutes, we have newspapers, magazines, books, plays, and movies to help us with a computer-type print-out of man's identity. The confusion grows with each new piece we read or picture we see. *How can a man be all those things?* How can a man *survive*—much less succeed —in a world with so many unreal, unattainable supergoals draped around his shoulders like an iron collar?

Before you and I can really *see* the man of today, we must be willing to examine some of the media myths and, with sound minds and clear eyes, probe, puncture, and demolish the unreal balloons of man's image in our world. Here are just four overinflated balloons which are full of hot air and unreal fantasies about men today. Oh, granted, in your town or your part of the country some of the balloons may not be the same color, size, or weight, but I'm sure somehow these ideas are flying, even where you live. You have been caught by them and, to some degree, you have undoubtedly bought their message. None of us has escaped the psychological messages of the media and to *some* degree all of us have been taken in.

First of all, according to the myths, in order to really be a man today you must be . . .

1. *Physically Attractive!* I do not mean you must be unusually handsome with a movie star's profile, but it's really terrific if you look like the men in the cigarette, wine, and car ads who have *physical, magnetic, and charismatic* appeal. Even if you look like a rugged, manly cowboy you are in; but, by all means, be physically attractive.

To do this you *cannot* be short, fat, or bald, to name just a few features which disqualify you. You must be tall— right at six feet or more. And it's good—very good—if you're built like a football linebacker. You *must* have hair on your head; and if you have a generous supply of the same on your chest, your manhood will not be teased or examined. While the chest hair can be matted down, the hair on the head must be styled and air-blown dry in a casual, yet precise way.

You may wear glasses now, as they have finally come

into vogue. They should be steel rimmed or genuine tor-
toiseshell and, preferably, the lenses should be tinted. At
this point in writing if you should be getting new frames,
as my husband is, you should try for the aviator's-goggles
look; however, that will probably be changed and out by
the time this book is printed.

As to how you dress—well, your Sunday-go-to-meetin'
clothes should either have the same exquisite tailoring as
those of Johnny Carson about to do the "Tonight Show,"
or at least they should have a casual air of elegance woven
through the fabric. Your grubbies can be a Hawaiian shirt
worn with walking shorts, black knee-socks, and oxfords,
or tee shirts with jeans and bare feet. But if you have any
class at all, you will abandon those getups for anything
from Arnold Palmer's golf shirts with knit slacks, silver-
studded western suits made of stretch denim, to racy paja-
mas and orange-colored jump suits a la Hugh Hefner.

If you drink, it doesn't matter what level you've
climbed to on the economic ladder of life. Whether you
are an executive or a hired hand, you must look attractive
while doing your drinking. You may be an alcoholic, but
your appearance must be smooth and controlled—like
the men-of-distinction liquor ads. If you "hold your liquor
well" you will be highly praised by your fellow drinkers.
This kind of admiration may blind you to the dangers of
alcohol, like the physiological effect alcohol has on your
body. The wife, the family, or the friend who has to cope
with the frightening, often bewildering, psychological
complications of drinking are victims, too. There is also
the ever-present struggle with the economic problems of
keeping a job, to name a few of the dangers associated
with alcohol. It is no accident that not *one* liquor or beer
advertisement or TV commercial ever shows or drama-
tizes a man falling down drunk in the skid-row section of
your town, driving a car into a child on a bicycle, or beat-
ing his wife and or children. The ads only emphasize with
verbal and nonverbal images a man having an absolutely

marvelous fun-time with the boys. If he is with a woman, she is quite lovely and *very sober.* They wouldn't dare show her otherwise because most women become exceedingly ugly when drunk.

If you smoke, you do it with sexy class and manly flair. The media tells you that you can have a beautiful girl come to your rescue, light a cigarette for you, and say with her eyes, "I wish you'd share your smoke with me." Or you can be a big boy and light your own. Either way, the trick is to look great while you're doing it. The ads never show a man with advanced emphysema smoking in his hospital bed. In the pathology lab of a large hospital near here (where they specialize in examining lungs after the patient has died of cancer) there hangs a huge banner which proclaims: THIS IS MARLBORO COUNTRY. We have been subtly brainwashed into believing we are *more* attractive while smoking. It is only recently that the American Cancer Society television commercials on the dangers of cigarettes have shown us believable pictures of truth as it really is!

To sum this up, whether you are a stockbroker or a drifter, if you have anything going for you which can be termed physically attractive—from the way you look, act, talk, or walk—you merit a high rating. Our society tends to regard you as more valuable than the unattractive or downright ugly man. It is a strong myth; yet as a man ages this myth declines a bit and gives way to others more high-powered, such as the next myth of credentials and the myth to end all myths, money.

If you're a little short on the physical appeal, you'll really need this biggie going for you. You must . . .

2. *Have Credentials.*   We have nearly lost our sanity in putting so much frenzied emphasis on the *expert* witness, the *professional* actor, the *union* musician, the *degreed* professor, the *doctorates* in the medical and scientific fields, and we turn a deaf ear to a man who doesn't have

such credentials or who doesn't meet our requirements.

In today's high level of performance, a child, even before he begins school, has just *got to be an achiever*. Mothers rarely brag about how long or how difficult it was for their child to walk or be potty trained. They don't tell you about the negative qualities in their children. More often they bore you silly with which child walked first and how fast they gave up diapers. We are eager to impress friends and relatives with *performance* (which is the name of the game) even in regards to our children.

We are a youth-worshiping culture, and about the only thing that takes a higher priority than youth is a youngster who is an early arriver. We laud the youngest to graduate in his class, the youngest to win in Olympic competition, and the youngest to be president of a corporation; our minds seem to compute the words *success* and *greatness* as we think of these youths. We have little patience (or none at all) with the slow learner, the late bloomer, or the thirty-five-year-old man without educational credentials.

If you are a professional actor, football player, singer, or you have a Ph.D. in nuclear physics, we will put you on a television talk show and ask your opinions on politics, marriage, or the current effectiveness of prisons and death penalties. Not only will you give us your opinion (which sometimes sounds like a great pooling of ignorance), but we will *believe* you! Because of your credentials (and it doesn't seem to matter that your credentials are in fields unrelated to the discussion) we listen intently as you boldly set forth your ideas.

If you are a man who is a professional or you have your master's degree or doctorate, we automatically class you as a better man, a bigger-than-life man, and a man of authority. When we take away the myth of credentials, it is sad to find that you may be an expert in your field of brain surgery, but you cannot for the life of you (or all your education) meet any of the emotional needs of your wife or family in your daily living together.

By now you may have decided I am against all handsome and degreed men. But that's not true. I'm simply sadly aware that we have made some of those myths such as handsomeness and having credentials into gods to whom we pay ridiculous homage. We bow and scrape before these gods. In fact these gods are so precious to us that we go to ridiculous lengths to appease them. If you can't earn your credentials by four, eight, or ten years of higher education, you can buy your own. You can pay for access to exam questions and answers, or you can skip that whole trip and send in your money with your mail-order form and obtain a phony degree. Then, if all else fails, you can wait a few years until you can convince some place of learning to gratuitously bless you with an *honorary doctorate*. I deplore this trend of giving honorary doctorates among some theological colleges and seminaries of today. But the gods must be worshiped.

There are credentials other than educational which are quite valuable and certainly rank high on our lists. One such highly overrated item is athletic ability. Because you are a male, you are *supposed* to be a sports achiever and you are spurred on to competition. Some parents force their young sons into the competitive world of children's sports long before they can handle the pressures, long before they are physically ready, and in some cases long before they are ever mentally or emotionally capable.

I feel badly for you if you were more interested in painting, writing plays, or playing the piano when you were a boy, especially if your father had sports credentials firmly in his mind. I know of one such young man whose father thought any interest other than an interest in sports was feminine and unmanly. The boy wanted to draw houses and dreamed of being an architect, but his father demanded that he be a baseball player. Now the boy is grown; having no confidence in his natural abilities to draw, he became a teacher, then a dropout, and now finally a civil service employee. Neither the father nor the son can talk to, accept, or forgive one another for life's early foul-ups. Both are miserable. The father bought the myth and the son has had to wear it.

Yet the balloon filled with the *achievement and credentials* myth continues to fly high.

The giant blimplike balloon, the one that devastates marriages and family units and relationships, is this next one. You must be a . . .

3. *Super-Jock Sexually.* Sex has been with us since Adam and Eve, but for the past decade we have seen and heard the whole world explode with the word *sex*. It is thrown at us from every quarter. We have experienced a 180° turn from Victorian no-no's and Christian silence to practically street demonstrations of how-to's.

Not content with mere sex between male and female, we now have graduated into perverted sex forms. Movies, books, and magazines are in high competition to see which can produce the most shocking display of sexual eroticism. We have this almost frantic urge to make sex come alive in living color and fill the air with its stereophonic sounds!

Not long ago, as I was shopping in a department store, the newest book on sex (with graphic sexual drawings) was displayed on a huge table, right in the center aisle of the store. Many of the books were on stands and open to their explicit drawings. I didn't have to ask a clerk if they had the book, and I didn't have to stumble around to some back counter to find it. I almost broke my leg over it! When a customer next to me noticed that both of our jaws were hanging open, she said to me, "In the middle of *this store?*" Both of us felt a little foolish because the myth says that there must be something wrong with us if those books and their drawings offended us. But I kept thinking as I walked away—in the middle of the store yet? I can't believe it!

Now, with such widespread availability and tons of written and visual material on the subject, we have to come

to the natural conclusion that people of our time know all
about sex. In fact, the myth says that the American male
is knowledgeable beyond belief and has hundreds of experiences to back up his talk. The myth has made you the
king of the bedroom. The myth, according to the *Playboy*
philosophy, has you having fun, fun, fun all the time, time,
time.

As a 100-percent American male you must prove daily
your masculine virility, and it's nice to be able to chat
about your high rate of sexual performance. Hugh
Hefner, the playboy of all playboys, is reported to have
bedded down with over 2,000 girls, making his sexual
escapades akin to the eighth wonder of the world. (Somebody's kidding us, folks.) However, if you are a bachelor,
you are supposed to live in a swinging-singles pad and
sleep with as many gorgeous girls per night as you can (or
are able). *Pleasure* seems to be the key word to all of your
sexual experiences.

If you are married, it seems perfectly logical and mor-
ally believable to have one or several standby girls available for sporadic and infrequent copulation when your
wife is out of commission, town, or both. Speaking of your
wife, she is to be beautiful, talented, and the world's most
marvelous mother to your handsome, brilliant children.
Most of all, she is to be completely understanding about
your sexual needs and desires, both with her and with her
competition. After all, this is the age of sexual awareness,
and we are raising our level of intellectual consciousness.
It is also a time for freedom and openness in marriage—
no matter what the marriage contract or tradition says.

After your first two marriages have failed (sometimes
you only have to go through one marriage and one divorce) the myth frees you to do your own thing sexually.
Then you've really got it made because the skies are the
limit. You can always fall back on the old cliché, "I tried
marriage and it doesn't work, so now I'm doing it my
way."

Your marital status, whether it's on, off, or in a stall,

brings me to the last and certainly the most important mythical balloon about men, for you must . . .

4. *Make It Financially*. If you, as a man, haven't made it in the physical looks department, didn't graduate magna cum laude with a Phi Beta Kappa key, couldn't qualify for an athletic scholarship, and your sexual reflexes are a bit slow—don't worry. If you have money, you barely need the other balloons.

Money is pure power in our world. With it you are everything; without it, nothing. Money makes up for every short-coming you have. You can be old, short, fat, bald, and possess as much sex drive as a neutered cat; but you'll be loved by just about everyone—unless, of course, the money runs out.

My friend Ron Cline once said that as babies we start out with the nonverbal attitude of *mine*. As we get to be two or three years of age, we learn the word *gimme*. Then after we move into adulthood, we live in the land of *I want*. As one young man so aptly put it, "All you need, man, is bread—you don't need nobody if you got the bread."

The pressure of making your mark financially mounts very soon in the big, bad world of commerce. If you don't cut the mustard just right, there is somebody standing off in the wings who is younger, smarter, sexier, and healthier to replace you.

I remember being interviewed by a television personality who was absolutely outstanding on her show before the cameras. She asked all the right questions of me, flawlessly moved from the interview to the commercial and station breaks, her hands never shook, and she was the most unflappable professional I'd ever seen. After the show I was fascinated by the total transformation of her personality. Nervously she chain-smoked one cigarette after another, screamed obscenities at her assistants, and told one cameraman, in short order, what she thought of his mother. When she turned and realized I had taken in the whole scene, there was an awkward pause before she explained, "I have a right to scream like this. There's a lot of money riding on me and this show, and right outside that door there are several younger, prettier, and more talented gals just waiting to replace me. All I have to do is foul up once and I've had it!"

Many a man has had that kind of pressure of performance shoved like a knife-point into his back, ever reminding him that, if he doesn't make it, the knife will slip on in between his ribs and he's done—through and finished.

This pressure can take a more simple approach. For instance, what is the first question you are asked at a party, office gathering, dinner, ball game, or a PTA social event? I'll bet it's one of these: "Ah, tell me, Mr. Smith, what do you *do for a living?*" or What is *your position* with this company?" All this really boils down to a simple translation which asks, "What is the source of your money, and how much of it have you amassed?"

The pressure isn't all from the world around us but very often comes from inside your own home as well. Even the most budget-conscious wives are going to the market, the drugstore, the cleaners, the gas station, the clothing stores these days and finding they can't begin to stretch the money to meet the needs. Our ever-changing economy is now pressuring you from within. Your wife buys one pair of shoes for one child and vividly remembers when she could buy socks and pants to match plus the shoes for the same money. She comes home to try to talk with you about prices and budget, but you have your own painful pressures to deal with—the house payment, car, utilities, etc. Many a fine *talk* blows up around you because you are both feeling the knife of pressures and each of you sets up your own defense tactics.

About then the beer commercial comes on TV and shows people having the absolute fun time of their lives. They seem to have no knives of financial pressure sticking

in their ribs, and the voice-over on the program says, in
a convincing yell-leader's tone, "You only go around once
in life—you got to grab all you can." We all get the message and think, "Yes, what the heck! I'll get more credit
cards, I'll send the wife to work, I'll pick up a moonlight-
ing job, and I'll make it so I can spend it!" Actually the
commercial is not very new, and the idea behind the
slogan was said thousands of years ago by the Prophet
Isaiah when he described the people of his day whose
philosophy was, "Eat, drink, and be merry . . . for tomorrow we die" (*see* Isaiah 22:13). The message of "grab all
you can while you can" becomes one of life's most con-
suming gods.

We buy the financial myth so well and so deeply that we
find ourselves either admiring or envying the beautiful
jet-set people—those people who seem to have it all
made. We watch them jet off to their beach, mountain or
Swiss chalets; we really believe we could be happy beyond description and relaxed if—if—if—only we had their
ton of money.

We are obsessed with the "when and then" concept.
"When I get a raise, *then* I'll like my job." "When I find
a woman who really meets my needs, *then* I'll be happy."
"When I get the break I deserve, *then* I'll show the
world." And on it goes. It is all too easy to continually
choose an illusive concept like "when and then" instead
of living out the reality of the here and now.

We are only mildly surprised when a millionaire's wife
commits suicide, or when we hear that the wife of a famous, rich man is a borderline alcoholic and has been
hospitalized several times in psychiatric clinics. We don't
dwell too long on logic as we ponder these things because
we always come up with the pat answer. "Oh, but with
their money they will work something out."

In my lifetime, I have seen the enormous emphasis on
financial success grow larger every year. People much
older than I, who have lived through all kinds of economic

ups and downs, are terribly concerned by the high priority placed in these times on the obtaining of money (legally or illegally).

We seem to have accepted money as the cure-all for every disease, need, or problem imaginable. A man who has not said one real thing to his wife in years shrugs his shoulders and says, "I don't know what she wants—she's got everything. She can go out and buy anything. She's got the house, clothes, and tons of *things.* What else does she need?" He has made the money, bought the myth, and paid for it. All he has to show for himself is a large brick wall made up of material possessions which stand solidly between him and his wife. He thought his money would buy a bridge; instead it has built a wall, but his intention and efforts were sincere.

You just know *if you have enough money* you can cure any emotional heartbreak and make up in material gains for any physical needs. All of us are disturbingly far from the truth, but because we have bought the myth we rush headlong into the quest for more money. Unfortunately, the image of glittering grandeur that money holds for most of us differs from the reality—money seems to be just outside our reach, and we never seem to get enough. No matter how much money we amass, we raise our standard of living to match it. So then we feel we need more, and it motivates our frenzied grasping for the security blanket of our society called *money.*

A friend who knew the international shipping and business tycoon, Aristotle Onassis, said of him, after his death, "Here was a man who had made himself *without* his family. A man who never had a successful family life because he couldn't, wouldn't, or never needed it.

"And then, when he did—after the death of his twenty-four-year-old son—Aristotle found himself in a position where his family was the one thing his enormous wealth could not buy. He had climbed to the top of the tree, but there was nothing there."

How terribly tragic. Here was a man who bought the money-power myth and ended up with everything and nothing. A case of mistaken priorities.

Thousands of years ago, Jesus asked the question, "For what shall it profit a man, if he shall gain the whole world, and lose his own soul?" (Mark 8:36 KJV).

Not long ago I wearily boarded a plane in the East, after a speaking engagement, and settled down to do several chapters of corrections on my novel *I Came to Love You Late.* I was so tired that I hoped no one would desperately need the Lord on that flight, so I could get the work completed in the three and a half hours I'd have. As I took my seat beside a tall, handsome man, I silently uttered, "Oh, Lord, if this man needs you, please find another Christian on this plane and *use them!"*

The man gave me a polite greeting and then (thankfully) he was quiet. I went to work and was totally caught up in my manuscript, even before takeoff. About twenty minutes into the flight, the man leaned over and asked, "What are you writing?"

Since I am asked this question on nearly every flight I take, I knew how the conversation would go, and I didn't want to stop working to discuss it. So, instead of my usual, "I'm a writer, and I'm working on a book,"—and the usual reaction, "Oh, I've never sat by an author before; what kind of books do you write?"—I skipped that; did not go into the contents of my books; nor, did I end with, "and I am a born-again Christian." I just cut across all details and said, "I'm writing a biblical novel."

He said, "I see." And I went back to my corrections. He ordered a scotch and soda. (To discover you are probably sitting next to some fanatical born-again Christian woman, thirty-six thousand feet up, and with the airplane's door closed is a terrible jolt to most people's nervous system.) I knew the man would not interrupt my writing now that he suspected I was "one of those." Right? Wrong!

In a very quiet voice, he leaned over and asked, "Doctor, can I contract the rest of this three-hour flight and tell you where I hurt?"

I turned, looked him directly in the eye, and decided he was very serious. I put my work away.

He began to pour out his story. Early on, though, I stopped him and said, "Let me guess. You are the head of some company . . . A hundred-or-more-thousand-dollars-a-year man?" He nodded affirmatively and then explained that he was resigning—even though he was at the top—because all the joy had gone out of his job.

I continued. "You've worked up steadily in this company, and you're on the top; but you've lost your marriage, children, the whole ball of wax. And now you've found some soft, young thing, twenty years your junior (He corrected me—she was only eighteen years younger), and you are really questioning what you have gained and what life is really all about!"

Essentially I had correctly described his life, and the bewildered, shattered man beside me really broke my heart. I could not control the instant springing up of my tears.

"Why are you crying?" he asked.

I was embarrassed by the tears, but I couldn't stop them. "I'm crying because your whole story is so sad. You have *wasted* the very best years of your life chasing after a myth, and now that you have caught it, you find your hands are holding thin air."

He responded with a soft, "Yes, that's true."

Then I chided him a bit. I said, "And I bet that somewhere in your family is a grandmother, sister, brother—*someone*—who has prayed for you every day of your life in the hope that you would find the Lord and give your life (dreams, desires, even work) to Him."

His eyes blinked in surprise, and he blurted out, "My mother. She's the one. She's prayed for me all these years."

We talked on. Finally, just before the plane landed in Los Angeles, he asked me for a list of my titles so he could read my books. He said he didn't know or understand what had happened during our conversation, but that something was stirring in his heart such as he had never experienced before.

I didn't give him the names of my books. Instead, I told him that I wanted him to read Chuck Colson's book *Born Again.* Briefly, I told him how similar his story was to that of Mr. Colson. He said he'd read the book. The plane landed. And I thought I'd never see or hear from him again. I learned a long time ago, on airplanes, that I am a seed planter—I rarely get to be a harvester—so I contented myself with the thought that Chuck Colson would be the reaper and that he would harvest this man's soul for the Lord.

Two weeks later, in my new post office box (I still don't know how he got that address), I found this letter. It started:

I am an unemployed $100,000-plus-per-year executive who is in the process of dissolving a marriage of twenty-seven years, and yet my heart is filled with "joy"—I'm experiencing a serene happiness that I have not felt for many years.

Good morning, Joyce.

If I have succeeded in gaining your attention, I will continue.

Friday, March 18th, you boarded a plane in Chicago, burdened by a manuscript that was due in January—expecting to be able to devote three uninterrupted hours toward its completion. Instead, you devoted that time to a traveler who was very much in need. You said the Lord put you into that chair for a purpose. Today I can believe that!

During the past twenty-five years of the "rat-race," the rags to riches success, the financial success, I had put aside my faith and my need for Him. Perhaps that is why it became so empty and so meaningless.

That Friday we met started, for me, with an unexpected blizzard in Buffalo, New York, where I had interviewed for a job the night before . . . I'm sure that it was a sign.

You should take a great deal of pride in your ability to communicate. Thank God you are gifted because it helped me to see and feel so many things. You were an inspiration. I came off that plane with a new thirst for life, and things began to happen.

In the rest of his letter, he describes how he left the plane and went to a Christian bookstore. They were out of Chuck Colson's book, but he bought seven of mine.

On the following Sunday morning, he did something he'd never done before—he turned on a religious TV program. It was Robert Schuller's church service, and not only was the sermon just for him (entitled, "How to Come Down from the Mountain without Getting Hurt"), but one of the guest speakers was none other than Chuck Colson. He spoke on "A Purpose to Live For!"

My new friend named the day—the day of his rebirth. A year later I got another letter from him—he had gone through with the painful separation and divorce; had married his new love; and, as he put it:

As to the future, we have broken ground to build our home and hopefully will remain here always. We will work together, build our business to effectively serve the community. We will work hard for worthwhile activities to help those in need, and *foremost*, we will endeavor to serve the Lord!

It is obvious that the blessings I have received far outnumber my return to Him in service. However, I'm sure that time will help me to be a better servant. Thank you, dear Joyce, for being the one to help open this new life!

That follow-up letter was a letter from a man who had truly found the Lord and, for the first time in his life, had discovered the true purpose and priorities of living. He is

a changed man—one who turned 180 degrees around
from the disillusioned, defeated man I sat beside on a
flight a few years ago. He trashed the myths of our society
and is living by the tried and true biblical principles—and
finding that a life in Christ really works!

As I said in the beginning of this chapter, these are just
four myths: Be physically attractive; have credentials; be
a super-jock sexually; and make it financially. They are
only a few of the misconceptions which surround you as
a man in today's world. There are many others, but these
are the real biggies. It is my hope and prayer that as you
read and check out all four, you will examine your own
life-style, your own beliefs, your own self-imposed handicaps, your own myths, your own strengths and weak-
nesses, and see if *you* have set up any false or unreal
standards to live by. Don't fall into the nation's number-
one habit of continually comparing yourself to mythical
fantasy concepts.

If you try these myths and compare yourself with them,
it will be easy to lose the real man you are. You will end
up trying to find the measure of yourself by using a yardstick made of soft wax. As long as the temperature and
climate stay right, the yardstick reads well, but as soon as
a little heat is applied, the measuring ability is dissolved,
melted, and gone. Under fire and pressure these myths do
not hold up. You must be wise in seeking out God's direction and you must be constantly separating fact from
fiction if you are to *be the man and not the myth.*

RECOMMENDED READING

DeJong, Peter, and Wilson, Donald R. *Husband and Wife*.
    Grand Rapids: Zondervan Publishing House, 1979.
Elliot, Elisabeth. *The Mark of a Man*. London: Hodder &
    Stoughton 1981.
Getz, Gene A. *The Measure of a Man*. Ventura: Regal Books,
    1974.
Vernon, Bob, with Carlson, C. C. *The Married Man*. Old Tap-
    pan: Fleming H. Revell Co., 1980.

3

The Decision Maker

> If you want favor with both God and man, and a repu-
> tation for good judgment and common sense, then
> trust the Lord completely; don't ever trust yourself. In
> everything you do, put God first, and he will direct you
> and crown your efforts with success.
>
> PROVERBS 3:4–6

We were just finishing dinner one night when the phone
rang. I toyed with the thought of ignoring it and letting
it ring, but since we had finished dinner and were just sort
of lingering with an extra cup of tea and talk, I answered
its urgency.

After he had identified himself, Norm Thiesen asked if
I would be available to speak to the entire male student
body of Biola College. He explained they'd never had a
woman speaker for men's chapel, but enthusiastically he
wanted me to come. I checked the calendar, found the
time free, and said, "I'd love to do it, but what do you want
me to speak on?"

He hesitated ever so slightly and then offered, "Well, I
guess what we'd like to know is this. What does a woman,
a Christian woman like you, want in a man? Our guys are
confused as to what a girl really wants or expects."

Instantly I thought of a dozen advocates of women's
lib who would give their right arm for an offer like this
one. Too good an offer to refuse! What a challenge! Just
think of the opportunity to speak before several hundred college-age men on *that* subject! A woman could
really let them have it as to what she expected from
them or wanted in them. I laughed and told Norm I'd
come speak on his chosen topic and I promised to go
easy on his men.

I was in the process of saying good-bye when he said, "Oh, Mrs. Landorf, I almost forgot—what will your talk be called? I need the title for our printed program." I was standing in our family room by the phone and, since the dining area is part of that room, I looked at my family seated around our evening dinner table. Our teenagers looked so dear. They were laughing about something my husband, Dick, was telling them and their faces were glowing in the warmth of love, laughter, and candlelight. My husband was every inch a man, a husband, a father, and a person of great character. I wondered what words would describe him, because I knew if I could find those words I'd have a title, not only for chapel, but for what a woman longs for in a man. At that instant my husband had reached the punch line of whatever he was telling the kids, and they all cracked up with laughter. Our son and daughter were coming unglued and the whole scene was heavy with great love. Somewhere deep inside of me I heard two words which described my husband perfectly. I thought, "I may not know about other women, but as far as I'm concerned. . . ."

"Norm," I said, breaking out of my own thoughts, "I'll call my talk 'Tough and Tender' because that's what a woman, or at least this woman, wants in a man."

A few months later I went to Biola College in La Mirada, California, and spoke in a chapel full of young men. It was a memorable time for me. It was the first time I'd ever spoken to a completely male audience; and, even though I honestly leveled with them, they rose to give me one of the most instantaneous standing ovations I've ever received. It was also the beginning of this book. I told the young men that long after I'd received Norm's call and replaced the receiver on the phone, I had thought about those two words—*tough* and *tender.* The words were at opposite ends of the poles, almost in direct contradiction to each other, yet toughness and tenderness must be central ingredients in a man if a marriage is to really get off the ground.

It was almost ridiculous—how could a man be at once *both tough and tender?* The two traits sounded as if they were in direct conflict with each other, yet were they? There in my dining room sat Dick, a husband and father who maintains a precisionlike balance between his ability to be tough with solid decisiveness on many issues of daily living and his gift of being a gentle, tender, and truly sensitive person who cares and communicates this generously to his family and friends.

Those who have known Dick for years know this was not always his gift, talent, or calling. In fact it has only been since we have become Christians, nearly twenty-five years now, that the traits of toughness and tenderness have surfaced, grown, and steadily developed to the finely honed point they now are. I filled up most of the book *His Stubborn Love* with the before-Christ Dick. That Dick I despised.

He was a stubborn, neat, computer-minded man. He was without compassion or genuine kindness. "After all," he rationalized, "you got yourself into that mess, now you work yourself out of it!" He was without tenderness to those who hurt and, while he loved the children and me, he found absolutely no avenue for expressing it. He paid the bills, did not drink, smoke, or chew (or run around with the girls who do). So he felt his actions and life-style said "I love you" well enough.

He was like the man I heard about the other day—a man who said of his wife, "Of course I love her, I pay all the bills, don't I? I don't know what she's all upset over. After all, I've given her everything a woman could dream of; house, clothes, and enough spending money to buy anything she needs or wants. What more does she expect of me?"

My husband was caught in the same myths that man and so many others submerge themselves in. He was attractive, he was earning his credentials and status symbols, he was sexy, and he was beginning to be successful. Since Dick maintained a good husband image, had the myths all in his favor, and minded his own business, he couldn't believe his marriage had disintegrated in five years and was over.

In those dreadful years one of the arguments we continually verbalized was one that started with my crying, "You don't love me anymore!" Exasperated, he'd reply, "But I do. Look, I do this, this, and this." I'd yell and tell him I wanted more than that, and he would counter, "You want more—what?" Because I couldn't put it into words —the vague feelings of everything, or at least something, being wrong—the argument always ended in our groping down a long, dark tunnel with no opening in sight.

As I related in *His Stubborn Love*, the day Dick had his honest, but rather desperate confrontation with God, it was a never-to-be-forgotten event. Dick became God-aimed. This is no easy trick. Oh, we are promised the Holy Spirit's ever-present help for daily efforts, the mind of Christ for wisdom, and a Bible full of promises too exciting to comprehend; but society's goals, myths, and unreal values are the nails of pressure which keep our hearts securely pinned down.

A man has got to aim himself—no, hurl himself—deliberately, intensely, and faithfully at God to be *God's man* if he is to survive the crisis of life. When Dick asked God to come into his life, forgive his sins, and make him the man God wanted him to be, that is precisely what began to take place. The process has never stopped, but it has never been easy to be God's man.

What is really astounding is that I never changed Dick into the tough and tender man he is today! I do admit to a small leaning to desiring a crack at it, but basically it was teamwork between Dick's willingness and God's ability. Wisdom for searching out real values and honest goals never comes from a nagging wife or critical children. A man does not change from his wife's or family's exterior pressures, but from a deep, powerful desire within him that is influenced, strengthened, and encouraged by God himself.

Dick would be the first to tell you that he has not arrived at his ultimate goals. In fact he does not expect to achieve perfection in this life; but what he has accomplished, what we have together, is nothing short of fantastic.

To think I almost missed this man! I almost succeeded with that razor blade in my wrist so long ago. I would have not only missed Dick, but our children, our marriage, and life as God intended. It all tends to boggle my mind. Dick is the same man who, back during the fifth year of our marriage, I hated with such vehemence that I refused him loving, understanding, real conversation, and any sexual pleasure just to get even with him for the hurts I felt he had rained on my life.

We both almost became suicide statistics that fifth year and we know now, had we succeeded in our attempts, our family unit would have been destroyed—broken relationships leave broken children. We had no basic values in our marriage. We were at a loss to decipher the difference between what was really important and what others believed important. Our pursuits of happiness were nothing more than misguided pursuits of status symbols and false myths.

Some years ago, listening to Dr. Paul Popenoe as he lectured to a class in marriage counseling, I found his comments to be most valuable. I was impressed by the amount of time he used in his talk to trace the histories of countries which had devaluated the position of husband and wife and did away with family structures. In nation after nation, as soon as the home went down the tubes, so followed the country. Wherever marriage and family relationships were ridiculed and finally dissolved, so went the nation.

I believe this is an accurate picture of marriage and family decay in our life-styles of today. The drums beat loudly and clearly telling us marriage is not for real or necessary—just a piece of paper—so why bother? Get everything you can, cheat whom you must, and grab happiness wherever and whenever you can get it—so goes the myth.

Sadly, this mad pursuit of personal happiness rarely finds its satisfaction. In every city, town, and country village across the world today, the bony finger of despair and depression will poke into the lives of children who are deeply affected by their parents' divorce. These parents are not necessarily unchurched, un-Christian people; the problem of divorce and legal separations touches both non-Christian and Christian marriages. I wish I could flatly say divorce is not happening in the church today, but the sad facts do not bear that statement into truth. I wish there were no Christian husbands leaving their wives for other women (or men, as is the case so much lately). But, in truth, never has there been such a high infidelity recorded among Christian men as there is today. A few months ago when a pastor was asked to resign his ministry because he was caught in adultery, another pastor remarked, "It is sad about that man, but I know of some twenty-five churches whose pastors are in the same situation."

Pastor Chuck Swindoll, in his book *Strike the Original Match*, tells of hearing about several highly committed Christian men who have left their wives. When he asked if these men—once respected in the Christian world as leaders, pastors, and godly laymen—seemed broken or had done everything possible to keep their marriages together, he was shocked at the answer. For he was told that there was no evidence of brokenness. In fact, most of these men had left their wives for other women and were still actively engaged in their Christian ministries—as if their acts of adultery, separations, or divorces never existed.

Once a woman phoned me and told me how her life had just exploded around her. She explained she'd just learned her husband had affairs with five of her best friends over a period of several years. That was the good-news part of her phone call. The bad news was, "He is a minister, and all of the women are in his congregation."

I wish it were true that good Christian husbands are not deserting their wives and children, but the facts, here again, just aren't so. Desertion is probably the best kept secret in the world of marriage breakdowns, but this year an estimated one hundred thousand men will leave their wives, families, and homes. For the first time in our history, the number of women leaving their homes by desertion will be almost even with the men's percentage, so the problem is not limited to men.

Many of these men and women will be good Christian people from good church families. As believers, we find ourselves asking why family desertion is becoming so much more in evidence. Some of the principal reasons for desertion are infidelity, drinking, and gambling. So far these are so-called non-Christian activities; but the next two on the list, in-law interference and irresponsibility, hit home hard because they really cut across the lines of Christianity.

The breakup in the home, the moral decay, the loss of love in relationships are huge puzzles. Puzzling us the most, however, is a marriage that looks sound, solid, and seems to be moving in a meaningful way; yet one day, out of the blue, it splinters into a thousand pieces before our eyes. My husband and I identify closely with this type of marriage because it's as familiar to us as a fading memory or a dream of what our marriage used to be.

The good husband is a respected member of his community and church. He has steadily provided everything for his family and, outwardly at least, he looks whole and well. Yet somehow inwardly, in spite of his outer suave confidence, his judgments, his values, and his ideals are unrealistic. He has allowed social pressures, unobtainable myths, and status symbols to dominate his thought processes. If he is pressured by his wife who has the same unreal goals, and if his family has bought the same myths, it can trigger this man into a psychic explosion that hurls him into the role of a dropout husband and father. He gives up and thinks, "What's the use, I'll never achieve my self-imposed goals, so why try?" These are men without a cup of self-worth to their name.

Marriages that have already gone under tear at my soul. Their tragedy can never be totally comprehended. However, the marriages that really get to the inner core of me and punch my heart into a flat, lifeless blob are the marriages that stay together in name and residence only. This type of marriage is one that lives on as an *emotional divorce*. It's a marriage where two people do not legally split but emotionally have nothing going for them; they live in a world void of love or understanding (as do the children of such a marriage).

The statistics can never be fully tabulated, but it is estimated by psychologists and marriage counselors that 75 to 85 percent of the couples in our country today live with emotional divorce. Because so many of this percentage are good Christian marriages, I am convinced that they live not only with an emotional divorce but with a spiritual one as well. (And who should know this better than someone who has spent five hellish, nightmare years drowning in an emotional and spiritual divorce such as we had.)

As I have already stated, coming to know Christ, as my husband and I did in our fifth year of marriage, was an exceptional event, but it was just the beginning. After the event came the *process of growing*—a process which I hope never stops or even slows down.

In those first early days of new life, both of us began to take a fresh look at goals and values, and it was then, so far back now, that the word *tough* came strongly into our thinking. It took the shape of words like: strong, solid, firm, robust, adhesive, powerful, and secure. We realized the character of toughness in a Christian man would manifest itself in certain ways. A tough man would be . . .

The Decision Maker. Having met Christ, I considered myself truly liberated to be the woman God wanted me to be; however, I'm not so dumb as to have missed the important fact of life that, whenever two people live together, someone has got to make the final, the last, the settling decision. I wanted a man who would accept his responsibility for being the *last word* man. I'm sure I had no idea of the tremendous pressure this puts on a man.

Consider some of the pressures and problems of your becoming a decision maker. What if your last-word decision turns out to be a complete flop—a failure or a mistake? It's a terrible shock to the system to go out on a limb, make a judgment, and find you've neatly sawed off the branch you're sitting on. So I discovered if I was serious about letting my husband be the decision maker, I'd have to be willing to reinforce my love to him and encourage him to continue, even after he had made an error in judgment. I had to let him know the "for better or for worse" clause in our wedding vows was in effect. If he failed, I'd be there willing to accept my part of the failure. This would take courage on both our parts; but Ephesians 5 was very clear about setting down some tough goals, and as we read it together we made some difficult commitments about who would be in final charge.

I recalled this moment in our lives in *His Stubborn Love* when I wrote:

I began to pray at great length about who would lead in our marriage, and each time it was as if the Lord said, "You're making too much out of all this; just do as I say, trust Me, and you'll see My way is right." Well, you don't just rush into making your husband boss—what if he picks up the nearest whip and chair and snarls, "Ah, ha! This is precisely what I have been waiting for." But the quiet voice was there and stubbornly persisting, sooooo . . .

I decided that if I could trust God's word about forgiveness, then possibly I could trust Him on submission and head-of-the-house stuff. I wasn't too sure, but I'd give it a try.

That night I said, rather haltingly, "Dick, I hate to tell you this, but I am going to make you the president of the Landorf Corporation." I said this with I-know-I'll-be-sorry-tomorrow written all over my face. But—guess who he made vice-president? That's right—ME! It was quite a surprise, and I was totally unprepared for it. How often we pray, just *sure* the worst thing will happen; and instead, a better, more glorious answer is given, and we feel like such monumental fools. How was I to know Dick was reading the same chapters? There is a lovely Scripture that reminds us: *before* we call He answers us.

Over and over Dick had read and thought about "loving your wife as your own self." It was dawning on him, brightly and clearly, that the first step to truly loving your wife was to love yourself. How to love oneself is another thing! Looking into the mirror one day he saw the face of a man who had been bought with a price; a man who had experienced a miracle; a man who, on some days, was not completely proud, but nevertheless a man who showed promise; a man . . . a new man . . . because of Christ. *He liked that man.* The rest was easy.

Our marriage definitely has the president and vice-president arrangement, and if this works so well in my husband's bank and in thousands of companies all over the world, think how well it works with both parties as one before the Lord.

The Landorf Corporation president never plans or executes moves without checking with his vice-president. On the other hand, this vice-president doesn't make decisions without checking with her president. There are meetings between us, and often the advice of the vice-president is taken and used, but it is the president who makes the final decision. Often the president will say to his vice-president, "You have more knowledge on this subject, so you make the complete decision." This doesn't detract from his position; quite the contrary, it makes him an even greater man. But HE has the last word.

I'm personally so glad that Paul qualified his statements about being a wife and a husband, particularly in the area of leadership. Notice how Paul tells me I am to submit myself to my husband—and then he uses a beautiful two-letter word—*as*. *As* I submit myself to the Lord (*see* Ephesians 5:22). He does the same thing again with husbands;

and while he tells you that you *are* the head honcho, he also uses that magic word *as* again and lets you know you are to be head of your household—as Christ in great love is head of the church. Neither you nor your wife were made to be wishy-washy doormats; but rather, in great Christlike love, you as the husband were appointed to have the final say.

I do not want to be quoted as saying my husband is the loving head of our house and then be guilty of calling all the shots and taking over in the privacy of our home. That merely emasculates him, and the last thing I ever want is to be a domineering woman who henpecks her husband.

During various social functions with a Sunday-school class or a group from the office, someone invariably says, "Let's get acquainted and we'll start by going around the room, each person giving your name, etc." During these sessions I wait for the painful moment when some man will say, trying to be funny, "I'm Helen's worst half," or "Helen's my boss," or words to the effect that he is just along for the ride. Old Helen manages everything and gives him visitation rights occasionally. He's henpecked and somewhere, sometime long ago, he quit fighting it and joined forces with her.

I am aware too, though, of some homes where the husband by choice has abdicated his role as decision maker. Sometimes he refuses to make a decision one way or the other because of the fear of being wrong. Twenty years ago he bought his wife a dress for Christmas. She took one look at it, told him it was the wrong color, the wrong size, and he must have been thinking of the wrong lady when he bought it. For years she wonders why every Christmas he says, "Take what money you need and buy yourself a gift." The fear of failure and her critical tongue keeps him from ever being the leader. My friend Keith Korstjens once said, "I'd far rather make a decision and be wrong than to be the kind of man who makes no decision at all."

Other men won't take up the decision-making effort,

particularly when it deals with disciplining their children.
Back in their childhood they had a dad who cruelly beat
them (out in the woodshed with a leather strap) for each
infringement of the rules. Forever in their minds had
been stamped the indelible words, "When I become a
father I'm never going to do that to my kid." When he has
his own children he lets his wife handle all the disciplinary
action. He stays out of sight while she assumes the bad-guy
role when action needs to be taken. He gets mad at the
kids for any number of reasons, but rather than disciplining the child who is responsible, he spends half an hour
yelling at his wife about *her* unmanageable son. He is
proud of the fact that he has never lifted a hand against
a child of his, but what he doesn't seem to see is that his
children have absolutely no respect for him. He has failed
to take a stand, and in the long run they have grown to
hate that quality in him. When his son is eighteen or
nineteen, appears to be turning out badly, and seems to
be going down for the eighth count, the father steps in to
spend some time with his son—only to find out it's too
late. The boy looks at his dad and says incredulously,
"Where were you all the time I was growing up?"

Facing issues and conflicts, and the rigors of decision
making are painful, but they are the true issues of life.
We'd all like to be freed from the task of leadership, but
a family is in deep trouble if the husband and father is not
in the leadership role. It's something that must be faced.

In our times, as in times past, there is that special grace
God has given to a woman who by circumstances of divorce, death, or default has lost her husband and may
have to take over all the leadership; but the best plan for
the family was to have male leadership.

The idea of male leadership bothers many of my
women friends. If I use the word *submission* in speaking
before a group of women, a large percentage have the
hair standing up on the backs of their necks. I know then
we are not talking about the real submissiveness of the

Bible. When a man fully accepts his responsibility as the decision maker and assumes leadership *as,* I repeat *as* Christ did for the church, life together with his wife and children works—really works. However, most of us make no effort to see how Christ loved the church, and very few of us relate it to practical, everyday living. For instance, how long has it been since you loved your wife enough to die for her, to be made a fool of for her, or to be embarrassed for her? That's the kind of loving leadership Christ showed for His bride, the church. Paul couldn't have chosen a better example for marriage and making it work. Show me a couple who has grasped this loving concept of the man leading as Christ led, and I'll show you a couple who is succeeding in their life together!

In her excellent book *Heirs Together,* Patricia Gundry talks about "mutual submission." She says, "Mutual submission is a way of living, an attitude toward others." And a few paragraphs later she states, "Mutual submission was a principle given to guide relationships between *all* believers." I understand so well what she means. Submission doesn't stand on its own two legs—it's got to give to someone else. It means submission to the Lord, submission to our mates, and submission to other believers. A Christian marriage folds up *without* mutual submission. Paul said it best in Ephesians 5:21 when he wrote, "Submitting yourselves one to another in the fear of God" (KJV).

If a husband really loves his wife as Christ loved the church, what woman in her right mind would not want to give herself wholeheartedly to that man? Any woman, that's who! Of course, the trick is to find a man like that! But a couple who has caught this concept is something else to see. The wife is no downtrodden shadow of a woman, she is not ignorant of the world around her, and she is not just another useful household appliance to be used by her husband when needed. She is independently strong, yet she is softly pliable; she's deeply aware and concerned for the world of hurts at her doorstep, she's

fully loved, and it gives her a built-in confidence that
nothing can shake. She may have a noisy, bubbly personality or a shy, gentle nature, but she walks with an unmistak-
able glow of radiance around her. In short, she's got it all
together. Her heart can safely trust her husband's faithfulness. She knows him well.

The husband is not forever seeking out the admiration
of other women. He is secure in the fact that he is loved
and respected. While he sees other women and is very
aware of them, he has no need to succeed with them; he
can enjoy the opposite sex without making them his quest.

This husband is not busy running around making half-
baked decisions. On the contrary, he is overwhelmingly
aware of what an awesome responsibility it is to be the
leader of a wife and family. He walks carefully, as if on
eggs, while making his family's important decisions; since
he and his wife are partners, made to become one flesh,
her opinion and evaluations are of the highest importance
to him as he considers all the problems and possible solu-
tions. When he does come to the final conclusions, he has
carefully checked out and weighed his wife's feelings and
words. Of course the planning works, because it's based
on the very way Christ loved the church. That kind of
loving takes a special brand of toughness.

Each husband and wife has to decide to decide. Since
every couple is gifted in various ways and limited in others, you must work out your decision-making areas in
practical ways to suit your marriage. For instance, in our
marriage we have decided to decide in these ways.

Dick decides when we need another car, what year and
make it will be and how much we can spend on it. I could
care less about those details, but the color of the car rates
a number one on my priority list, so I decide the color
(unless it's a used car and I have no choice).

When something is broken, Dick decides whether he
can fix it or take it out and have it mended. I'm no good

at all in the handyman department so we have rightly decided that Dick makes the decision here. Some women are absolutely gifted when it comes to repairing an electrical outlet or a broken water pipe. If your wife possesses those skills, kiss her twice—once for her ability and once for me! (One woman I know never loses her femininity or soft, beautiful glow for one second, but she can fix any machine in an entire office if it breaks!)

In the matters concerning decorating, painting, and what color and kind of carpeting we have at our house, we have decided that Dick's color sense is hidden somewhere in his toes, so he lets me decide which shade of blue is suitable for the upholstered chairs and which length of carpet shag will be best for our purposes.

The social calendar at our house is my responsibility. My husband has asked me to see to dates, dinners, and engagements. He has the final word, but this is my department. We check schedules together, but I am the one who suggests a time for the theater, a quick dinner out, or a time for after-church fellowship in our home.

None of these things are really important issues to you, I realize; however, I've included them here for you to catch a glimpse of how practical decision making can be, and what a lift it can give to marriage.

I know of a couple where the husband absolutely excels in flower arrangements (at one time he was a florist). His wife never arranges flowers because they have agreed it's one of his skills. Another couple has a wife who is talented in vegetable gardening, but is a poor cook. They have agreed that she grows the food, but he cooks it. He's a great chef. You may be better at keeping the financial books (a disaster left in my hands), so finances should be done by you and not your wife, but many a wife excels in this area.

A woman, any woman, longs for this kind of leadership in the home—one of balance where she knows her opin-

ions are regarded higher than anyone else's, but where
she can trust her husband's choices to be emotionally consistent in doing the very best for his wife and family.
When a woman sees her husband is using his leadership
and decision-maker position to build and strengthen the
home and to support the marriage, there is no way of
stopping or even slowing down her willingness to submit.
She's yours; you have her complete allegiance, plus a marriage that zings.

One of the most penetrating sermons on the necessity
of leadership in a marriage was preached one Father's
Day by our former pastor, Dr. Edward Cole. It was titled
"Fading Fathers," and it dealt specifically with husbands
who had abdicated their responsibilities of leadership. He
talked about children who become warped without male
leadership and ended by pointing out that the whole nation shows the effects of the warping. He was right on
target; at one point he spoke directly to the men of our
congregation, "Your wife and children might be completely surprised if you suddenly take over the leadership
of your home. Most women (after they have regained
consciousness) will be thrilled by this new tack." He had
us laughing, but his point went all the way home. I
remembered that, when Dick became the loving head of
our home, loving me as Christ had loved the church, I
found myself admiring and respecting the leadership
quality I had been so afraid of before our conversion.

You may ask like so many women in my meetings,
"Joyce, do you believe in being a submissive wife?" My
answer, based on my husband's brand of leadership, is a
resounding—yes! But keep in mind my yes is because of
Dick's faithfulness to being the husband God wants him
to be.

My husband's love and attitude toward me is like his
own opinion of himself. He is not an egomaniac in love
with himself, but he does not hate himself either. His
self-worth, now reclaimed by God, is intact—complete—

especially since his sins have been forgiven. He can honestly look into a mirror, like himself because of God's forgiveness, and turn around to love me beyond my hopes.

The man who is a decision maker and a leader no longer presents the image of a stubborn, overbearing man; he is a *tough* man, dedicated to being *God's man.*

SCRIPTURES

Decision Maker	Ephesians 6:10–17
	Colossians 3:10, 11
	Galatians 5:16, 17
	1 Corinthians 7:20, 24
	Psalms 37:23, 24
Self-Image	2 Corinthians 3:18
	Galatians 6:4
	Hebrews 13:5b
	Proverbs 28:13
The Tough Life	Ephesians 3:17–19
	Proverbs 20:24
	Proverbs 3:5, 6
	1 Timothy 1:19

RECOMMENDED READING

Butt, Howard. *The Velvet Covered Brick.* New York: Harper & Row Publishers, Inc., 1973.

Dobson, Dr. James. *Straight Talk to Men and Their Wives.* London: Hodder & Stoughton 1981.

Swindoll, Charles R. *Strike the Original Match.* Eastbourne: Kingsway Publications 1983.

4

The Spiritual Leader

> But if you are unwilling to obey the Lord, then decide
> today whom you will obey. Will it be the gods of your
> ancestors beyond the Euphrates or the gods of the
> Amorites here in this land? But as for me and my fam-
> ily, we will serve the Lord.
>
> JOSHUA 24:15

It is part of our humanness to want to hear the words of
a dying man, in fact whole books have been written on the
subject. Our interest stems from the idea that if a man is
dying his last utterances will be of great significance. One
of the best books along this line is *Voices From the Edge
of Eternity* (compiled by John Myers). Indeed many last
statements are very notable and revealing.

Jesus, dying on the cross, issued His enduring, last
words, "It is finished," and it was the promise of all promises come true. We, who would be called by His name,
were assured by His dying statement of *life*—real life,
here and now, and life forever after death.

The last spoken will and message of the Old Testament
giant Joshua challenges my heart and mind today as I
write this chapter on spiritual leadership. In the twenty-
third chapter of his book, Joshua tells the leaders of Israel,
the elders, judges, and officers, "I am an old man now"
(*see* v. 2). He then traces all that God's hand has done for
them during his long life as their leader. He instructs
Israel to carefully follow God's laws and reminds them of
God's faithfulness toward them. Tenderly he adds, "So be
very careful to keep on loving him" (v. 11). In his next
statement Joshua changes subjects and moves into a practical statement on marriages, warning the people not to

intermarry as God will not protect them if they do. Finally, he says with untroubled acceptance, "Soon I will be going the way of all the earth—I am going to die" (v. 14). Then, in chapter twenty-four, we hear Joshua's final words to us. Near the middle of his message he makes his most significant point by going to his favorite theme, and he is eloquent beyond belief. He tells Israel that serving God should be the highest priority of all life. Then he asks them to choose, that very day, whom they would serve. His key statement comes when he says, "But as for me and my family, we shall serve the Lord" (*see* Joshua 24:15).

I could just kiss that darling old man. He never said, "I, Joshua, will serve the Lord." He defines and strengthens the statement, takes upon his shoulders the responsibility where it has been laid, and says, "As for me and my family, we shall serve the Lord." He told the whole nation that day, once and for all, of his tough, unyielding decision to obey and serve God with his life and the lives of his entire household for whatever time he had left. He never implied that Mrs. Joshua would handle the spiritual chores in his family's condominium. He took the reins in his own hands and clearly knew the road he'd take.

Somehow Christian men have forgotten Joshua's fine example and have stepped back to let their wives take care of the spiritual chores as well as the other household tasks. They seem to feel that developing personal family prayers and devotions, getting dressed and going off to church and Sunday school, and daily building a love of God in the hearts of the family is mere women's work. Men seem to simply abdicate and withdraw when it is time to pray or counsel with each other. Many a woman I've talked with in the last five years alone has said, "I'd give anything if John (or whatever-his-name) would pray with me."

Your wife may be absolutely starving to death spiritually because you are not willing to be the tough, consistent high priest of your home and family unit. You shrug your shoulders and say, "Well, all that's woman's work," or "I don't know how to pray," or (and this is classic) "I'm a man of few words and all that religious stuff is personal anyway." And so you slip off into the welcome oblivion of your work, schooling, or hobby as easily as butter slides off a hot knife. Vaguely you hope that by merely attending church, joining the choir, or becoming an usher, it will appease your wife (and God) and give your children the Christian training they should have.

Most of the time it doesn't work out too well. For instance, just about the time your children hit the tornado-like times of their teenage years, they begin getting into one mess after another. You feel you can't cope or understand their behavior because, "After all, I've raised them to be good Christians." By that, you really mean you have gotten up on Sundays to go to church because of your wife's insistence; you have prayed at the table and said your little standard—"Dear Lord, bless our food and us four, bless us now and evermore"—and precious little else. Since you've never been the spiritual pacesetter in your home, and real Christianity is being lived and practiced reluctantly for one hour on Sundays, why should you be surprised when your children's faith in God is shallow and holds up under the teenage years of pressure about as well as a thin sheet of ice across a deep pond?

Forgive me if I sound too harsh and come across as being hard on you, for I don't mean to stomp you to death over this, but someone has got to dare to say it. Someone, even if it's only me, has to run out as if on a busy freeway and yell, "Hey, you guys—you're on the right road, but you're going the wrong way." The tone in my voice is not edged with indictments against you and my finger is not pointing in an accusative way, but rather there are tears stinging my inner soul. Furthermore, I am not alone. The women of today's world cry with me, "When will our men, our dearly beloved husbands, take the prayer, the Bible reading, and the counseling of spiritual problems in our homes as *their* challenge?" Or they ask, "When will they even accept a partner's responsibility—joining me—as we, together, become God's people?"

Men, if you feel this kind of responsibility is absolutely above and beyond your abilities, let me quickly assure you: *God, the One who sees all hearts and understands all limitations, honors His Word—and your intentions.* You don't have to accept this responsibility alone.

One guarantee came when Paul and Silas were talking to their jailer and fellow prisoners. They were asked by the jailer, "What must I do to be saved?" The two giants of the faith answered, "Believe on the Lord Jesus Christ and the Lord will save you and your entire household" (*see* Acts 16:30–32). That verse was written to you, to all men and for all mankind; God wasn't kidding around. As I just said, He is a God who will honor His Word and your intentions.

I have often had occasions to wonder just how fast I would have come along in my spiritual life had Dick been unwilling to take spiritual leadership as he saw God's leading. I have an idea that without Dick's efforts, his pacesetting in spiritual things and his continually seeking God's will and direction, I might not have had the strength, willpower, or courage to continue as a Christian woman. I'm fully aware that my attitudes contribute to the healthy or unhealthy mental state of my entire household, but it is the husband's responsibility to give spiritual and emotional security to his family unit. Many a woman, stronger than I, has given up in her obedience to God because of the weary, constant struggle with a husband who would not, could not, or did not allow God to develop his spiritual assignments.

If you, as a Christian, are a secret Christian—one who down in the depths of your heart has asked God to forgive—but you have never told anyone on earth of the decision, and your wife and children only suspect your status, there is marvelous news for you. You can come out of hiding and take your stand!

First of all, you've come into a fortune—and I doubt if

you had just won on the million-dollar lottery ticket you'd keep it a secret—so hear me out. Romans 8:16, 17 assures us that God's Holy Spirit speaks deep down inside us and whispers His confirmation that we are God's children. This you already know. But next comes the line, "And if children, then heirs; heirs of God, and joint-heirs with Christ . . ." (v. 17 KJV). So there you have it: you have won the lottery ticket to end all lottery tickets! I may be *The Richest Lady in Town,* but you are definitely the multimillionaire man of your community! Never lose sight of that thought. There is a slight catch, however. You've heard the good news, so now I'll lay on the bad-news part of this newfound status. We are very clearly told by Jesus Himself in Matthew 10:32 (RSV), "So every one who acknowledges me before men, I also will acknowledge before my Father who is in heaven; [Then, here is the scary catchphrase.] but whoever denies me before men, I also will deny before my Father who is in heaven." So it seems to me the beginning point of being a spiritual leader starts the second you publicly state your intention and position as a Christian man—*before others.*

"Oh," but you say, "I don't have to tell my wife I'm a Christian, go 'forward' in a church service, or be baptized or sprinkled in water while the whole world looks on. I can just decide inside. After all, this is a personal matter. I don't think it's anyone else's business." In light of Jesus' own words, I'm sure the decision to be quiet about one's faith is a *decision for denial* and it would be sad for a man to finally stand before God at the end of his lifetime and hear the heart-chilling words of God, "Depart from Me— I've never known you."

The Bible does not tell you that after you become a Christian you should go out, set up roadblocks in your neighborhood, stop each car, bus, or tricycle, and tell people you are a Christian; but it says simply to *acknowledge* whom you have chosen to serve in some way—to some other human being. Start with your wife!

I'll never forget Dick's statement of choice when he came home, took me by my shoulders so many years ago, and solemnly, sternly, and without hesitation stated, "Joyce, I don't care what you think or say, but today I made up my mind. I am going to be a Christian. I mean a real honest-to-God Christian—a Christian husband and father" *(His Stubborn Love)*.

It was the moment he took on a newly discovered ministry, without ever going to seminary, without any knowledge of Greek or Hebrew. He chose his pulpit—our home —and began his ministry as our high priest. It was also trial and error all the way! Dick didn't know how to be the spiritual leader any more than you may know right now. All he *did know* was that God *intended* for him to do it; so, blindly, he began. He brought God's spiritual security into our lives and it never went smoothly. However, his determination paid off.

The song "People" from *Funny Girl* is one of my very favorite songs. The songwriter wrote that people who *need* people are the luckiest people in the world. Although I do not believe in luck, I do agree that we need others. We need someone's love, someone's approval, and someone's comments. We need each other like a singer needs an audience; and, preferably, the listeners should be people who can't carry a tune but adore music passionately. (Ah, what a concert is given under those circumstances.) We need each other physically and mentally, but *spiritually we desperately need each other*.

Almost twenty-five years ago, when we were brand new babies in Christ, Dick's first decision, spiritually, was to find us a church. He felt a church would have to have three important functions. I am amazed how, even in those fledgling moments of his new life in Christ, his spiritual judgments were so sound. We had to find a church for us to worship as a family, to serve as a family, and to fellowship as a family. The criteria set down served us well for over twenty years. Just recently, when Dick

was transferred to a bank in Palm Desert, we moved from
the Pomona area and once more found ourselves visiting
churches. Finally, to our joy, we found just the right
church; and we did so by using the same tried and true
guidelines.

I remember, though, when we were still new at finding
God's will, we did things *very* simply.

We listed the churches in our area. There were thirteen
or fourteen, any one of which might be a possible church
for us to begin our new lives. We made Sunday visits until
we had attended each one. (A lesser man than Dick might
have given up, as it was a terribly frustrating job.) Finally,
as we talked it over, we said we'd join the church that said
to us, "We *need* you both." We knew I'd be recognized
as I'd sung in churches since I was thirteen; but I didn't
want to join a church if they did not want or think they
needed my husband. This whole thing of settling in a
church was his idea, anyway. I remember telling him
there was just one church in our area, "the big white one
on the corner," which I didn't think God wanted us in. I'd
had some bad experiences with that denomination, so
went to all the other churches and ignored "the big white
one on the corner."

People recognized me—as we knew beforehand—and
then Dick would tell them we had just moved into this
area and were looking for a church home. We'd listen to
their replies but never, in all thirteen churches, did we
ever hear, "We need you both." We were somewhat discouraged.

Then one Saturday our newspaper announced that one
of my favorite trios was to perform at "the big white one
on the corner." I swallowed my prideful statements, and
Dick drove us to that church. It was a large church, but
there was an unusual warmth in it. The music of the congregation was enthusiastic; the trio (all artists I knew and
recorded with) was great; and the minister's sermon was
direct, practical, and soul-searching. Dick said, even be-

fore the service ended, "We are coming back to visit next Sunday."

After the final hymn was sung we walked down the aisle to say hello to the trio, but were stopped by one of the pastors who bounded off the platform. We listened in stunned silence as Rollin Calkin said, "You are the Landorfs, Joyce and Dick, and these must be your children. My, we need you both in this church." I thought, "For crying out loud, Lord, not this church!" But Dick said, "Yes, we'd love to be a part of this church and we'll be back next Sunday."

My husband's decision began a fantastic ministry in our lives through that church, its pastor, its music, and its host of *real friends.* His decision made possible a substantial part of our children's religious training and provided the Christian security they so desperately needed in today's world of shifting mores.

Several times during these past years I have talked with a Christian artist or minister who has just gone through a divorce. When the appropriate time has opened up, I have asked one strategic question which would go something like, "I know you sang and spoke at churches around the country like I have done for ten or more years. But, tell me, what church did you consider your home church? The one your children went to while you were on the road?" The answer was generally pretty much the same, "Well, we were so busy in so many churches, we never joined one. No, our children didn't go regularly."

Each time I've heard that tired excuse as an answer, the wheels of my heart have slowed with sadness like they were rolling ever deeper into heavy mud. We need to experience a time of worship to God in His house, to tithe a tenth or more of our income, to give Him gifts above our tithe, and to hear the singing of the choir and congregation. We need to be warmed by a friend leaning over our pew who whispers, "All week I've been thinking about you and have been holding you up in prayer before our

Lord." We need the message that streams forth out of the
heart of our pastor, and we *need* the presence of *each
other* if we are to survive another week.

My husband had become the spiritual pacesetter of our
house in choosing a church home for us, but it began to
be more involved than that. Choosing a church was just
the very first step in being the people God wanted us to
become.

I suppose tithing our income was the toughest spiritual
decision Dick was ever to make. I mean—touch a man's
wallet, particularly a banker's, and you've put your fingers
on his heart and pulsebeat. Financially, there is no *right*
time to begin to tithe. You are never at a place where you
will not *feel* tithing. We were no different from anybody
else in our early tithing days. In fact we had just started
our regular giving when my husband lost his job, found
another one, and took a salary cut.

Early on, in our Christian walk, Dick gave "tithes" to
the church after all bills were paid. Usually it was not a
tenth of our income, but just a small scrap or token. However, he began to feel a little guilty about "holding out on
God" in the light of how extremely well our personal lives
were going. True, we were Christians who had been in
church a good deal all of our lives, for one reason or
another; but our marriage, since we had really accepted
Christ, made a fantastic turnabout.

Materialistically and financially things weren't too
swift. We were surprisingly happy in spite of beans and
hamburgers and not having one extra dime left over each
month. We knew it had to be God working the changes;
it seemed only right that we give Him at least what the
Bible said should amount to a tenth of our income.

At first nothing happened, but Dick began writing out
the tithe check *first* after payday. Then he wrote the bills
and did the bookkeeping. Neither of us remembers when
the joy hit, because it was such a subtle thing. But somewhere in those early, rather sparse years of giving, tithing

phased from duty to a quiet gladness. Our income was very low so tithing was painful; strange as it seemed, we always had a place to live, and we never ran out of money or food at the end of the month. True, there was absolutely nothing left over for years and years. After paying our tithe to God off the top and not the bottom (even when we had hospital-emergency bills) we saw all needs met.

It became very exciting to pay God first and watch in ridiculous, silly joy as everything else fell into place. In the following years, our income increased; so did our percentage of tithing and our extra giving. Now we have experienced the truth, as someone a long time ago expressed it, *you can never outgive God.* The incredible verse in Luke has come true so many times I dare not take the space to give you examples, but it's one of God's most fantastic promises. "For if you give, you will get! Your gift will return to you in full and overflowing measure, pressed down, shaken together to make room for more, and running over. Whatever measure you use to give— large or small—will be used to measure what is given back to you" (Luke 6:38).

I remember reading a newspaper story which told of a man who was suing his church. He claimed he'd paid one-tenth of his income for three years and had never once received any blessings in return, as the minister had promised. (He was overlooking the obvious blessing—the one that concerned the fact he had a job and was well enough to keep it—a blessing that many people don't have.) As I read the story I remembered the main reason for tithing and the Bible reference in which the pastor may have found his promises, Malachi 3:7–12. The prophet is telling the people how they have robbed God and what would happen to them if they really tithed. "Bring all the tithes into the storehouse so that there will be food enough in my Temple; if you do, I will open up the windows of heaven for you and pour out a blessing so great you won't have room enough to take it in!" (v. 10). We serve a God who is still faithful to His promises. I don't care if the man is suing his church. This same God is a master financier. He very plainly says to invest in Him and He will see to your increases. Your stock will go up and your financial rewards will astound you. What a thought —God is my stockbroker. In these scary economic times, who better could I find?

We realized, during our early years of Christian life, God did not need our money, even though He asked for it; but rather we needed the great experience of giving and sharing with God. Once we began tithing we found that God blessed our lives in three ways: We had financial wisdom—to our surprise; we had paying investments; and we had an open opportunity account which taught us to use what we had, not what we wished we had. We were to learn too that God, His church, or His ministers were not out to get our money because when God has the man, He automatically has the man's wallet. Giving gradually becomes a trip into the miraculous.

Daily Bible reading—both individual and with the family—began too. When the children were in the six-to-ten-year age bracket, family devotions did not mean an hour of Old Testament reading after dinner. (We never had the hour to begin with.) What it did mean was a quick (not more than seven minutes) reading from the book *Little Visits With God* by Jahsmann and Simon. The reading was interspersed with remarks, questions, and a very informal, unrehearsed dialogue with each other. At one point we had neighborhood kids dropping in to join the devotions. They heard us laughing and wanted to know what was so funny. Their parents never believed for one second we were really studying a Scripture verse.

As our children grew into their teens we began reading short excerpts from the Bible's new translations and paraphrased editions because those writings spoke to our kids.

As Ken Taylor so aptly said of the Living Bible, "If this paraphrase helps to simplify the deep and often complex thoughts of the Word of God, and if it makes the Bible easier to understand and follow, deepening the Christian lives of its readers and making it easier for them to follow their Lord, then the book has achieved its goal." (Adapted from the preface to the first edition of *Living Letters*.) As I stated in *His Stubborn Love:*

Rarely are we formal at the devotions time, and we've encouraged our children to add comments or ask questions any time they care to; they often do, and we've found it to be a time of instruction, yet filled with gentle fun.

As to personal devotions, a woman (if she does not hold a full-time job) has more opportunity to read, pray, and study God's Word. However, please take note. I did not say she has more time than a man—only more opportunity. We never find the time to pray, we always have to make it and take it, whether we are a husband or a wife.

While our children were growing up, my husband's Bible reading was confined to the after dinner sessions. Now that the children have gone, he reads in the morning while he eats that awful dry stuff he calls cereal. But his prayer life has never known such limitations. From almost the moment we really started this process called growing in Christ, Dick took on a new spiritual ministry. He accepted his God-given opportunity to be a praying man. Like tithing, it never came easy; always, even to this day, praying means shutting off or putting down something else to make time for it. Tough job? You bet!

When I was proofreading this chapter to my husband and daughter, Dick interrupted my reading to tell me I should say something about all those times a husband needs a wife to gently say, "Honey, we need to pray about such-and-such." He went on to remind me how the pres-

sures of his job get to him and preoccupation with those
pressures sometimes dulls his praying ministry. "Over the
years," he continued, "I have responded when, without
nagging, you have said, 'We really need a time of praying
together.' Never once have I said, 'No, Joyce,' but I did
need the gentle prodding to maintain these years of praying together."

Since Dick is a man of few words, he found that in his
personal prayer life he was better equipped to remember
the needs in our lives if he had a record of written requests. So early in the development of our Christian lives
we began to see the incredible influence our little spiral
notebooks had on us, our friends, and our children. Both
our children, Rick and Laurie, are married; but occasionally, when they visit us, they still peek and check our
prayer lists to see if they are on them, and to take our
spiritual temperature, as it were.

When Laurie was seventeen she began to be very
aware of her parents' prayers. Dick kept his notebook of
written requests with him in his car and on his way to and
from work he would talk to the Lord about each item. It
was one of those beautiful times of praying without ceas-
ing even in peak-hour freeway traffic. (The old Bible
adage to "watch and pray" might well have been said for
freeway drivers who drive while praying.) In *The Fra-
grance of Beauty* I told of Laurie's experience in checking
out Dick's list. She had driven his car somewhere and read
his list—Bank assignment: Northern California? Joyce's
new book. Laurie dating Don. Bank audit this month.
When she read her name and her date's name, she ran a
line down the page and there, in her beautiful printing,
was this addition:

Dad,
   I thank you with my whole heart for praying for Don and me.
There are times when I become so frustrated in our relationship. [He is a marvelous young man but has not had a real
personal relationship with Christ as Laurie has.] I pray you and

Mom will try to continue to understand. You both are terrific parents. You have helped me to know the difference between right and wrong.

I love you, Daddy, and you are always in my prayers.

Love,
LAURIE

A few pages later, there was an addition.

Good morning, Dad,

I will be praying for you this morning. Please keep praying for me. My heart is burdened for Don. I never realized how much I could care for and like someone, but the difference of him not being a Christian is so great. I realize that he's in the Lord's hands, but sometimes it's so hard.

I thank God each morning for you. Have a good day at the bank.

I love you, Dad.

Love,
L. J.

"Teach them to obey everything that I have commanded you. I am with you always even unto the end of the world." Amen. P.S. I hope you don't mind me writing in *"your"* prayer book.

Neither Dick nor I minded, but as Dick said, "It's awfully hard to read her words and then drive the freeway without tears blurring your vision."

Without this little book in Dick's car, we might have been denied a look into our 17-year-old daughter's heart. How beautifully the Lord helped her share her innermost feelings so we can really "zero in" with prayer over this situation. After all, what better gift do we have to give her than our specific prayers? (Incidentally, Laurie broke up with Don the very next week after writing the last entry in Dick's book. Since he was not a Christian, they just did not have enough in common.)

Cover your own list with your hand after you have prayed over each entry, and then thank God for working each problem out, for giving each answer, and for showing His loving will in each circumstance.

He is the same yesterday, today, and tomorrow, and your list will be just one more proof to encourage you.

While Dick's personal prayer life has seen many God-answered miracles, I suspect our prayer life together as partners has been the most rewarding. It has given us unexpected dividends and benefits we never, never considered when we first began praying together. Now, I wish I could tell you that right from the second we became Christians we had a marvelous prayer life that was completely satisfying in every way. That statement is a long way from the truth, and that's not how it really happened.

We were novices at praying *separately,* much less *together.* Fumbling and embarrassed as he was, out-loud praying was essentially painful for Dick. My noisy nature allowed me a bit more freedom in out-loud praying, but it was remarkable how easily Dick went to sleep while I prayed. (Of course we had the added hazard of having our prayer time together just after we went to bed, but it was the only time we could make for prayer.) While Dick prayed I found I could mentally redecorate the bathroom or let my mind wander to any number of projects. It's no wonder we soon lost interest in this boring concept of prayer.

We might have missed forever the most enriching time of our lives had it not been for a flight to San Francisco I took with Dr. Ralph Byron. He is a famed surgeon at City of Hope Hospital in Duarte, California, and a man who is equally adept at performing surgery in an operating room as he is at teaching the lesson on Sunday to his class in church. Dr. Byron was the speaker that night for a banquet in San Francisco and I was to provide the special music for the program. I remember sitting next to this great surgeon and thinking, I know he has just got to have a vital prayer life with Dorothy—but when? He was in surgery before dawn every day and not out until afternoon. He did many speaking engagements in the evening, yet I just knew he prayed with his wife! I was sure of it so I blurted out, "Dr. Byron, just *when* do you and Dorothy pray?"

He smiled and answered, "Just before we go to sleep at night."

"But," I questioned, "doesn't one of you go to sleep before the other finishes?"

He turned in his seat, looked directly at me, and got to the heart of my probing with—"Ah, I see you and Dick are not praying the right way." Perceptive rascal, that doctor.

"Okay, I give up. How do you pray the 'right way'?" I asked.

There on that plane, thousands of feet up in the air, Dr. Ralph Byron gave me one of life's most valuable lessons on prayer. Those lessons came from a spiritual giant of a man—a man who wants, above all, to be God's man; and the things he taught me that night have turned our prayer into one of the most beautiful times of our lives.

"Dick," I shook him out of a deep sleep. "Honey, I've got to tell you what Dr. Byron told me about prayer to-night." He couldn't wake up completely, but he was aware it was 2:00 A.M. and I was home safely from the airport.

"Mm, that's nice, honey, glad you're home, see you in the morning," he mumbled. I pestered him into a wakeful but blurry-eyed awareness and he said, "Okay, give me the plan and we'll take ten minutes' time to pray, and then I'm going back to sleep."

Forty-five minutes later he said, in a surprised way, "Why did you stop so soon?"

Dr. Byron had suggested we take turns each night at being the leader or introducer of requests. This night it was my turn and in one short sentence I introduced and prayed very conversationally for subject number one. Then Dick prayed a short sentence for subject one. Next

I introduced and prayed on subject two and Dick followed. We repeated the process until we had covered
about seven items. It had been so interesting, so like talking with God in a three-way conversation, we had both
completely lost track of time. Our ten-minute limit had
jumped into forty-five flying minutes!

The next night it was Dick's turn to introduce the requests of his heart and within a week several strange
things began happening. First of all, at dinner one night
I said, "Well, how did it go at work today?"

Dick had matter-of-factly answered, "Oh, just fine." But
later that same night, when he introduced subject number four, he prayed, "Lord, help me to know how to
handle George and the serious problems he's creating at
the bank."

My first thought was, "For Pete's sake—George who?"
Then I realized what Dick could not share at the dinner
table (or in any conversation with me) he felt perfectly
free to present by prayer to the Lord. I remember praying intensely for old George what's-his-name that night
and being just thrilled that Dick had shared a real need
in his life. (Even if it was in a sneaky, roundabout way!)

Next we began to notice that on my night to give my
requests I would pray for Dick's requests. On Dick's night,
many of my concerns would show up on his lists. The bond
of love grows deep when we see our partner caring,
remembering, and praying for our need and our request.
I'll never get over the first time, on my husband's night
to introduce requests, he ended his prayer time by praying, "Lord, thank You for my dear wife. I love her so
much. Give her a good night's sleep and great day tomorrow. Amen."

If, after so many years of marriage, you can fall in love
all over again with the same person, that was the moment
for me. How strange it was—there we were praying together because we knew we should (almost like a duty);
but suddenly we found ourselves, because of prayer, fall-

ing deeply in love with each other. I remember quiet
tears streaming down my face in the darkness that night.
I had heard my husband tell God how grateful he was for
me and that he loved me. It was the most romantic thing
he'd ever done, and if you think romantic things are not
important to a woman, you're enrolled in the kindergar-
ten class of the school for understanding women.

Whenever I've taught a seminar on *Tough and Tender*,
this section on praying together has brought the most
vocal response from the men. Over and over I have listened, as a man from my audience has shared, "My wife
has been after me for years to pray with her, but I never
knew *how."*

In my mail I've read, "My wife and I didn't wait until
we got home to pray like you taught. We decided to pray
in the car, as we drove home, just to see if it would work.
When we found it did work—I pulled off the road and
God really met us there!"

Another man eloquently wrote, "We've been married
eight years and we are Christians, but I've never been
able to convince my wife (now that's a switch) that we
should pray out loud. After hearing you, I asked my wife
to just try praying once more with me, but in this new
way. Reluctantly she said yes, and what happened has
been a miracle. Having a pattern to follow, but keeping
it simple, freed her from what she 'thought' she ought to
be saying. She no longer feels guilty about being shy or
having very little formal education. I praise the Lord for
this unaffected way of talking with the Lord and each
other."

If I could wave a magic wand for you in regard to your
prayer life, I would wish several very important things:

1. *Make the time, in the ideal place, for conversational
prayer with your wife.*   It does not always need to be the
same amount of time—your needs differ from day to day
—but take whatever time you need. It's important to

keep our vertical channels open to God as well as our horizontal communication channels open to each other.

2. *Keep your requests simple, honest, and liberally sprinkled with genuine thankfulness.*

3. *Listen to your wife's requests with all your hearing ability.* She may be giving you many clues as to her emotional and spiritual temperature. You may hear much more than verbal intonations and this may be one of the very best ways God has in mind for you to understand her inner tickings. (You know, her inner workings that are such a mystery to you.)

4. *Ask God to give you a keen sensitivity to know when to drop everything and right-then-and-there pray aloud.* I mean this for your wife's and your children's prayer life as well.

Once when I was in Georgia, I had been stranded by a military chaplain. I was alone in a hotel and without plane reservations. I phoned collect to my husband. All I said was, "Dick, I've just been dumped off after my speaking engagement, I don't have flight reservations, it's raining and. . . ."

He broke into my running disaster report and said, "Dear Jesus, my wife is 3,000 miles away. I do not understand the mix-ups and why she is left alone, but I ask You now to calm her. Lord, take care of her right now, give her that quiet peace that only You can give and do for her what I cannot do today. Bring her quietly and safely home to us. Thank You, Lord, right now for what You are doing. Amen."

Even before he finished my hysteria left; then we calmly discussed flight plans, what to do about my hotel bill, etc., and all was worked out. It didn't stop raining, but my husband had prayed *instantly and out loud* for me, and my confidence in making plans was restored.

If you ask God for this kind of sensitivity, He will give it to you even when you are not in times of crisis—like the night of our son's wedding. Dick took Rick aside in the basement of the church and they both prayed together for God's blessing on Rick's about-to-begin marriage. A few years later, on Laurie's wedding day, we both took her out of the bridal room and, in an outside hall, we had a special time of prayer together. She told me the other day that the moment spent there is one of her favorite memories. Those "special moment" prayers were preceded by thousands of ordinary prayers, and these times of praying together became the reinforcement rods of our family life.

5. *I would wish, too, that you would be real in praying.* Consider "said" prayers (memorized, repeated prayers) and prayers which are just a nice collection of rhetoric as just simply not where praying's at! Your wife needs to hear you pray—honestly from your heart. She needs to see you cry over the heartaches of people around you, and, most of all, she needs to feel your love of God. All this can be accomplished through your praying together.

6. *Before you pray, check out your attitude and treatment of your wife.* Peter, that outspoken individualist and rugged fisherman, suggested rather strongly if a man was having trouble praying and his prayers weren't too effective, he should examine how he was treating his wife. It's surprising to read Peter's subtle yet blunt pronouncement of, "You husbands must be careful of your wives, being thoughtful of their needs and honoring them as the weaker sex. Remember that you and your wife are partners in receiving God's blessings, and if you don't treat her as you should, your prayers will not get ready answers" (1 Peter 3:7). *Evidently the blessings in your life depend on your treatment of your wife as your partner.*

Being the spiritual leader means being a spirit-filled man who commands in love, who teaches in love, and who respects others in love. Actually, its the old Joshua-policy of choosing this day whom you will serve and saying, "As for me, and my family, we will serve the Lord."

SCRIPTURES

Spirit-Filled Leader	1 Peter 4:8
	1 Corinthians 13:3
	1 Corinthians 16:14
	1 Corinthians 6:3, 4
	Romans 8:6, 9, 14, 16
	Psalms 37:29–31
Direction for the	Psalms 25:4, 5, 8, 9
Spiritual Leader	Psalms 37:5
	Psalms 37:34
Giving	Numbers 18:28
	2 Corinthians 9:8
	Malachi 3:10
	Philippians 4:11–13
	Matthew 23:23
Praying	Romans 8:26, 27
	Psalms 130:3, 4
	Matthew 6:7, 8
	Matthew 18:19, 20
	Hebrews 13:18, 19

RECOMMENDED READING

Benson, Dan. *The Total Man.* Wheaton: Tyndale House Publishers, 1977.

MacDonald, Gordon. *The Effective Father.* Wheaton: Tyndale House Publishers, 1977.

5

The Exceptional Listener

Dear brothers, don't ever forget that it is best to listen much, speak little, and not become angry. . . .
JAMES 1:19

According to most psychologists and marriage counselors today the biggest stumbling block along the hazardous road of marriage seems to be made out of our inability to talk or listen to each other. Since a *marriage without communication cannot survive,* I think you can understand why I feel compelled to write about it. The purpose of this chapter is not to overwork the subject, but we must never forget that communication is the oxygen that keeps marriages alive and breathing.

One of the very best books on the subject is one aptly titled *Communication: Key to Your Marriage* written by H. Norman Wright. He has wisely stated that God has created marriage for at least three great reasons.

1. Companionship
2. Completeness
3. Communication

I find his three reasons extremely right on target. As a woman I see these three things as the highest goals on my priority list for my own marriage. Item number three keeps items one and two in working order and its importance cannot be denied.

Talking with each other started out simply enough when we were about two years old. As we grew older we added more words to our vocabulary, began to understand and comprehend terms more readily, and generally felt we could talk quite well by our teen years. Most of us entered adulthood with a small dose of smugness, for we were confident that communicating with others was no big deal.

If you are like me, though, it was a sad and rude awakening to find the doors of communication firmly shut after a year of marriage. I found when loving, honest communication stopped, it sealed my husband and me off from each other. Our verbal expressions clogged and choked in our throats, and we were reduced to using nothing more than meaningless clichés. In retrospect we found that the lack of talking and listening had preceded the death of our marriage by years.

For several years Dr. James Dobson and I teamed up to speak on marriage and family relationships, in seminars all over the country. From that time on I have often been involved in marriage counseling.

Sometimes after a couple has shared their trouble spots with me I ask them this question, "Can you pinpoint a time or event when one or both of you stopped feeling and caring for each other?" They generally bypass the question a bit, but their answer usually involves communication.

The wife says, "We used to talk for hours when we were dating, but he stopped talking to me once we were married."

The husband retorts, "I'd listen to her if she actually said anything, but I hate all that small talk."

The wife cracks back with, "That small talk you just described is about your home and your children. Don't you care about them?"

"Sure, I do," he continues, "but you're always yakking at me, and it's just easier to turn you off."

You see, talking is only one-half of the popsicle; the other half is listening. Communication is a combination of both.

Since most of us see ourselves as pretty good talkers, ready with just the right groupings of words, I'd like to spend time on the listening part of communication. I pray this chapter will open some long-closed doors between you and the woman you love.

Listening in marriage is to be savored like a wine connoisseur tasting a rare French wine or a gourmet diner inhaling the aroma of a delicately flavored stew. Neither the wine nor the stew is to be gulped down and swallowed in selfish indulgence or hurried impatience. It is to be savored and enjoyed.

In one house we had, I decorated a wall in the family room with 8″ × 10″ pictures of each member of our family. Laurie's picture showed her holding our dog Sidney; Rick and Teresa were shown in our living room; my picture was taken outside by our roses; but Dick's picture was my favorite. It was just a shot of his head. His chin was resting in his hands and he was looking away from the camera. Actually, we were talking at a table during a friend's wedding-rehearsal dinner. The bride's brother-in-law spotted Dick and, using his telephoto lens, he snapped the picture from across the patio. I absolutely loved the shot because I was the one to whom Dick was so ardently listening. I've seen that interested, loving look a hundred times, and it was captured on film for me to cherish always. It was a portrait of loving communication, even if it was only the listening half.

Listening is almost a lost art. It's as tough as making the decisions and being the spiritual leader of your house, but it can be done. Here are some areas to examine and probe involving your listening attitudes and habits.

1. *Have you already stopped listening?* Your wife may be a compulsive talker. Was she always that way, even before you were married? Or did she just seem to get that way with time? Some women talk at the moment of birth and a steady stream follows each moment of their lives forever after, but others have developed a nonstop flow of talk for other reasons. Many times a compulsive talker

is really shouting to be heard by someone. The more
bored you look, the more you yawn, the more you watch
the dog or TV, the harder she talks. She just talks all the
more to compensate. You may have stopped listening a
long time ago, and she knows that better than anybody.

Do you think this has happened to you? When was the
last time that you asked these questions of your wife?
"How do you feel about . . . ?" and/or "What happened
here at home today?" Do you ever intersperse her remarks with, "You may be right, Hon"? If your wife feels
you are not willing to listen to her, she has two options;
to talk louder and harder; or to talk less and withdraw.
Either way, it's very hard on the marriage.

Just last night my husband asked me how I felt physically during my speaking engagements in Seattle the day
before. When he asked the question he looked directly at
me (ignored the dog) and quietly waited for me to answer.
He was giving me all the go-ahead signals to talk. I didn't
feel threatened by someone else capturing his attention.
His eyes were on me and his mouth was closed. I knew he
was listening, and not just to my words but to the real
message I was trying to convey. I gave him the facts, but
I sensed he was after more than facts. He was really after
my feelings. I was free to sit back and explain those feelings in unhurried detail.

Whenever we *listen for feelings* instead of information,
we are on the way to being real listeners. A wife longs for
even a few minutes of a husband's time in real listening.

2. *Do you listen without presuming or judging?* The
man who hates his wife's small talk is a man who presumes
he knows everything she is going to say before she says it.

In one of our seminars a man asked me how he was
supposed to accept his wife because she was "so dumb."
I asked him if she was a good wife and mother and he
answered, "Oh, she's pretty good but she's so stupid I
can't believe it." I listened to him and suggested that

maybe she had other qualities he could find. I recommended that he list all her good traits next to her bad or weak traits and then see which list was longer. Finally he should examine his own heart as to which was really important to him. After the day-long seminar had finished, I was talking with a very attractive, blonde young woman. She told me in an articulate way how Dr. Dobson and I had helped her. She mentioned a number of things our seminar had taught her, and I was impressed by her heartfelt gratitude as well as by her ability to express herself. Just at that moment the man who had told me earlier of his "dumb" wife came up, stood beside the woman and said, "This is the one I was telling you about." I could hardly believe my ears. His wife was far from dumb. I could only conclude that years ago he must have assumed she was stupid over something, turned his hearing aid down (or off) to her feelings, and didn't have the slightest idea of what a fine, bright wife he had.

We not only presume to know what our mate or children are going to say, but we also judge their conversation before their last word is uttered. There is a verse in Proverbs which says, "What a shame—yes, how stupid!—to decide before knowing the facts!" (18:13). Yet we are guilty of such stupidity.

Have you ever gone to a basketball game and sat through the first, second, and third quarters with no scoring by your team? Have you ever left ten minutes before the game ended because you just knew your team had lost? If you have, then undoubtedly you have had the experience of hearing later the news that in the final seconds of the game your team won by a point or two. You missed it because you prejudged the outcome before the final score was tallied. We do this same thing all the time in listening.

We use the words, "Oh, you *always* leave your clothes around," or "You *never* show up on time." We shut off our hearing and decide we know what will be said. (It's very

easy to do this with children; if one does it often enough
the children will refuse to share anything by the time they
are teenagers.)

I've just named two killers of listening and communicating. Here are some others.

"I *know* that!"

"Let me tell you something!"

"I'm sorry but. . . ."

Now, here are some builders of verbal and nonverbal
communication.

"I'm sorry."

"I was wrong."

"I love you." Add with these

    Direct eye contact

    A touch or an embrace

    Or even a simple nod

and you have an uncomplicated pattern for listening
and talking. But it takes real toughness and self-discipline
to be *hearing listeners*.

3. *Do you ever listen by touching?* Listening is not always done by the ears; sometimes it involves holding or
touching.

Over and over, as our children were growing up, I
hugged Rick or Laurie while they wept. Sometimes I
knew the exact nature of their conflict, other times I had
no idea. As their sobs subsided, I did not ask, "What's
wrong—why the tears—what's happened?" It was
enough to hold them, smooth their hair, and just *be there*.
Just as many times as I recall my holding our children, I
can remember Dick walking into our home and my running to his open arms. What a way to listen, to care, and
to feel with someone.

After our infant son David died, I was recovering from
a Caesarean section and went to my doctor's office for a
postnatal examination. I had not seen my doctor since

David died and I'll never forget our meeting. It was soon after surgery so Dick had brought me to the doctor's office in my nightie and robe. I was very weak and the nurses helped me up on the examining table. Then everyone left me alone to wait for the doctor. When he came in he said absolutely nothing. He did not give me a phony, cheery greeting. He merely walked over to me and very tenderly put both of his hands over mine. I looked up at him and with teary eyes he turned his head to the window and continued to hold my hands—but he never *spoke* a word. What he communicated in those brief seconds spoke volumes to my heart. It even brought a measure of healing, because I knew he deeply cared about my loss; yet nothing was said then or ever.

Sometimes when your wife is frustrated beyond belief over a rebellious teenager, a critical remark made by a relative, or maybe by an extra job—try touching. I'm suggesting you give the touching and holding technique a chance. It might really show her *you do hear her,* and *she may hear you* better than she's ever heard you before.

4. *Are you communicating in honesty?* We all talk and listen at different levels of honesty. It was John Powell who outlined for us the five levels of communication which most of us use daily. In his book *Why Am I Afraid to Tell You Who I Am?* he listed these:

Level 5—Cliché Conversation
Level 4—Reporting the Facts About Others
Level 3—My Ideas and Judgments
Level 2—My Feelings and Emotions
Level 1—Complete Emotional and Personal Truthful
         Communication

Most of us are pretty good at Level 5 with its no-risk policy in effect. You can't get too hurt by saying, "Hi, how are you?" But getting down to Level 1 requires real honesty. Sometimes if we are open and honest we are rejected by the other person, and often that's too big a risk to chance.

One of the things I hate the most each day is getting up. Naturally I'm married to a man who is God's gift to the morning. (Opposites are still attracting!) I don't care if Dick is an early riser, I just wish he would leave me alone. I spend most of the morning mumbling under my covers, "Don't bother me." Dick tells me my tombstone is going to read:

> JOYCE LANDORF
> BELOVED WIFE AND MOTHER
> DON'T BOTHER ME!

When Dick was assistant vice-president of a bank in Pasadena, California, he was put in charge of an elaborate breakfast for the staff. It was for his forty employees—and I was his assistant chef. That breakfast meant cutting and seeding thirty or forty cantaloupes, buying pancake mix, syrup, juice, sausages, etc., the night before, and getting up before the crack of dawn to get to the bank before 7:00 A.M. We had a delicious breakfast by 8:00 A.M. and it was a huge success. Gals who never eat pancakes ate Dick's perfectly round jobs like they were going out of style. Even now they still talk about that breakfast. I'll never forget it either!

I had not met any of the people at Dick's bank. Five of his top assistants arrived early. As I was introduced to each of them, the script read like this:

The first man said hello to me and then made a comment to Dick, "It's really nice your wife got up so early to help with this, etc." Dick rhapsodized, "Yes, it certainly is! Usually this time of the morning all I ever see is the back of her head." Ha-ha. Everyone laughed—even me.

Second man: Same greeting, same remark and same comment from Dick. Ha-ha. Everyone laughed. I smiled slightly.

Third man: Same. Ha-ha. Everyone laughed. I didn't.

Fourth man: Same. Ha-ha. Everyone laughed. I withdrew.

Fifth man: This was ridiculous and unnecessary! Ha-ha. Everyone laughed. I burned one pan of sausages!

Now, since I had been trying to get up with Dick (most mornings), I was really fit to be tied at his funny (not very) remark. I had several options: I could forget his remark—no way! I could use my tongue and give him thirty lashes right there—not too swift an idea. I could cry or throw the pan of burned sausages at him. I gave this sincere consideration, but both seemed too messy! I could wait and talk with him later—this I decided was best.

However, discussing a conflict often involves risks, if you're really going to be honest. I was hurt and feeling very embarrassed about Dick's comments when they happened; but later, by the time I got home, I'd cooled off a bit. Now, here's one of the problems about conflicts; given enough time we often shove them under the rug. We think, "Oh, I won't bring it up, after all it was a small thing." However, if I do that, I find myself going back to that rug and mentally poking around under it. The problem stays very much in focus that way.

If we are to communicate in honesty, we are going to have to wait for the best time and then present our feelings. Timing is very important. We must not store all our little grudges in gunnysacks and hold them too long, for *held grudges* become too large to handle.

The evening after the breakfast there wasn't an opportunity to talk with Dick, but the next night when he got home from work, I took the big plunge. "Dick," I said, "I have to talk to you about something."

He said, "Sure," and went on shining his shoes.

"Honey, I know this is trivial, but yesterday I was very hurt by something you said. In fact, you repeated it four times after you said it, and I find I'm still smarting under it."

"What did I say?" he looked up in boyish innocence, making me want to drop all charges (but I told him, anyway).

After I repeated my sad story, he stopped polishing his shoe, looked at me and said, "That's right. I did say that, didn't I? Oh, Hon, I'm sorry. I didn't mean to hurt you at all."

I was a little taken aback by his instant apology but I responded with, "I accept your apology. Thank you." The matter seemed settled, but because I had been very hurt and more than slightly embarrassed by his remarks I said, "Maybe we need to talk a bit about my getting up and your attitude about the issue. Maybe there's more at stake here than we realize." And there certainly was.

What followed was an important dialogue for us. I learned that my getting up with him seemed to set the tone for Dick's entire day. When I made breakfast (even a bowl of cold cereal and juice) and walked with him out to his car, he felt he could face the arena of his office. Dick was sustained by my quick prayer in his car as he started the motor; somehow my smile (sleepy, at that) was a warm memory all day for him.

We arrived at a reasonable solution. Dick would not say anything to me on the mornings we both knew I needed to sleep in (after a late banquet, or if I was ill). But on the days when he really needed me and my moral support he would say, "I need breakfast." Without a grumble I'd get up—no matter what.

This communication—honest and painful to some degree—was handled in nonabusive language; the language which says, "I know this is wrong or silly, but I feel such-and-such and I need to talk with you." It is also the language of lovers. Two people who have earned the respect of each other have the right to have a kind, loving, open honesty with one another. This vehicle makes it possible for them to work out the conflicts of their hearts. The key to nonabusive language, though, is making sure you discuss the problem. Do not attack the person, because all that does is destroy his feelings of self-worth. When he sees his self-image being destroyed, he becomes hostile and defensive. Then all you've got is a rip-roaring argument with both parties flailing away at each other in hot anger. Stick with the issue at hand (don't confuse this issue by digging up old issues, either) and leave out the personalities as much as possible.

I'll never forget building a little foot-high stone, decorative wall at our Casa in Mexico. I wanted it to be a beautiful wall, but Dick wanted it to last forever. We gathered stones, mixed cement, and started the wall. It almost killed us both. We were working at opposite ends of the pole over that wall. I kept finding odd, pretty-shaped rocks; Dick kept saying no and grabbing up the big, solid, ugly ones. We were about to come to blows over that silly wall. Finally we dropped down to Level One of communicating and began to nonabusively and honestly tell each other what we wanted in the wall. Dick compromised his standard for strength and I came down in beauty. I'm sure the wall isn't as strong as he'd like, but it's sure a bit more creative than he intended. I love looking at that little stone wall because we built it—together. It took some doing but we did it, and the wall stands as a tiny monument to nonabusive language.

The same thing is true about communication. Whether you're building a wall or a marriage, you have to talk and listen in open, loving honesty, using the nonabusive language of love. How do you talk and listen this way?

a) *Slowly.* Pick your time wisely. Don't try to talk out a conflict when it is in the heat of happening. During the building of our wall we stopped, had a quick lunch, and then talked out our goals for the wall.

b) *Honestly.* Share your real feelings in humility and share a little background as to why you feel that way. Admit your feelings may be wrong or silly, but share them.

c) *Patiently.* Ask what you can do to help the situation. Let the other person know you are willing to correct, change or apologize to straighten this conflict out. Do not expect or demand miracles overnight!

Now, here are the last three areas of listening for you to examine.

5. *Do you communicate through written words?* Talking and listening are certainly forceful tools of communication, but sometimes the most meaningful tool is that of writing.

At our house note writing has been a family tradition, not only for communication but for survival as well. It has considerably lessened the strain of keeping track of everybody. On the phone (that seemed the ideal place in our house) has always been a note from the missing member of our family. All it said was where, what, and when.

They have been: short, "Mom, I'm at work. Love, Rick"; desperate, "Mom, please stop everything right now and pray for me. Today is a rough day, Love, Laurie"; and sweet, "Hon, you must go to the bank today. Love, Mr. Dorf." Dick's handwriting, however, leaves so much to be desired that usually by the time I've figured out what he wrote—it's too late. The bank has closed! I've been saving these notes for years, and they are a running narrative of a family loving and laughing.

The notes that please my heart the most, though, are the ones I find tucked away in my suitcase whenever I travel. The first rule for me when on a speaking engagement out of town is to check my luggage for notes. One May I was speaking in the East and, as usual, a search of my luggage produced two large envelopes. Dick and Laurie had both written, "Do not open until Mother's Day." Laurie had added, "On the other hand, if you are really tired, depressed, and need a lift, you can open this any time."

As you can see, I'm big on note writing! Before I leave on a trip, Dick gets a note on top of his pillow in our bedroom. If I've run out of time to write a long, smashing love letter, I merely write, "Get that other woman out of here by Saturday because I shall return!"

Each time I begin writing another book, I'll find somewhere, in my yellow tablet of paper, a scrawled note from Dick. It reads, "Write a good book, Darling, I'm praying for you!" And it never fails to give me the added surge of confidence I need.

If I am near Dick's office building, I'll stop and leave a very sexy, unsigned note under the windshield wiper of his car. That has proved interesting—especially when he has had to drive a client somewhere for lunch that day.

Once in a while the mailman brings me a letter from Dick. Neither one of us is out of town; but my husband, at his office, has penned a few words to me, and the envelope contains a ton of love.

My secretary Sheila said, "I used to work with a man whose wife mailed a hysterically funny card to him at the office every Friday. We all looked forward to Fridays!" Smart lady, that wife, she knew the value of the written word. Cards, cartoons cut out of the paper, or just a small heart drawn on a piece of paper with your initials on it can say so much. In fact if you are a man of few words, this might be the ideal way for you to increase both your vocabulary and her love for you.

I regularly cut cartoons out of newspapers and magazines and send them to the person that I deem most appropriate—my husband, children, in-law children. Even my dentist gets all the medical cartoons I can find. They are expressions of love.

6. *Are you a gut-level listener?* The great Dr. Elisabeth Kübler-Ross, who has studied many terminally ill patients and has written the book *On Death and Dying*, told this story on a television interview not too long ago. It involved listening, not with ears and mind alone, but with one's "guts" as well.

Dr. Kübler-Ross told of a terminally ill young girl. The

staff did not know if the girl knew she was dying and most
of their attempts to lead her into a conversation about it
failed. The girl was very near death and yet she could not
speak of it. She was a very compliant patient, easy to
handle, and never demanded anything. The nurses were
a little surprised when, in the middle of the night, she
urgently rang her call button.

A nurse quickly answered the call and came in. The girl,
lying under a plastic oxygen tent asked, "What would
happen to me in here if the hospital caught on fire?" The
nurse just smiled and answered, "Oh, you'd be all right,"
and started to leave the room. However, just as the nurse
got to the door her "gut-reaction" (as Dr. Kübler-Ross
expressed it) responded to what she'd heard. The nurse
turned around, walked back to the bed, unzipped the
oxygen tent, and crawled onto the bed. Holding the girl
in her arms she asked, "Would this help?"

She heard the girl's real message, "I am afraid because
I know I'm dying." She heard it somewhere deep inside
her soul and intuitively responded with loving care. The
girl died shortly after, but she was not without comfort.
The nurse had listened for the real meaning of her words.

We all come so close to missing what people are really
saying around us. Sometimes it's too much work, too
many pressures, too many fears or risks involved, and so
we do not listen with our gut-level intuition.

It is a precious gift to give to your marriage if you can
listen to your partner with all your soul. My husband,
through the years, has presented me with this gift many
times. I remember the time he made me smile in spite of
the conflict, because he was so *right on* about really hearing me.

I was in a hurry, fixing dinner, and trying to pull things
together. First I told the dog, in no uncertain terms, to
get out of my kitchen. I did it so loudly he disciplined
himself, crawled into his bed, and stayed there twenty
minutes.

Next I called Laurie and said in a very whiny voice, "Do you think you could possibly put the ice water in the glasses?"

Last, I snapped off the news on the television set as Dick was watching it and said, "Dinner's ready—I don't want it to get cold." (Dinner, as I recall, was not too thrilling, but at least it was warm.)

Later that same night, as I slumped down on the couch next to Dick, he folded up his newspaper, took my hand and said, "I sense that the chapter you're writing is not going too well."

What made me smile was the knowledge that I'd said *nothing* about the book I was writing—good or bad—yet that was the very source of my rude, impatient behavior.

His first two words, "I sense," were like stepping into a warm, relaxing bath after a whole day spent fighting a war on a battlefield. I leaned back into his arms and just breathed out, "Thank you, Honey, for understanding. You're right, it is going badly, and I'm sorry for my stupid behavior."

We spent the next hour talking about this book and I was encouraged by my husband's loving words to continue writing. It would never have been possible without his gut-level listening and his words, "I sense that you. . . ."

7. *Do you take time to listen?* How much time do you have in dialogue with your wife each day? Probably not as much as you think.

In a recent study by Cornell University 200 fathers were asked to estimate how much time they spent daily with each of their children. The men estimated they spent an average of fifteen minutes per day per child. Then the children were fitted with tape-recording devices, and the actual time was clocked. The final studies showed that the average time each man actually spent with a child per day was thirty-seven seconds!

If there were a way to conduct the same study on husbands and wives, I wonder what the length of time would be? Each couple needs to find the *sharing time* of the day. Ours happens to include a couple of times, but the first one is just after Dick gets home. Our children are grown and they are not climbing all over him for his attention, so the first twenty minutes are mine. Dick changes his clothes and shines his shoes. Generally I stand around waiting. I lose five minutes of dialogue this way, but men need a buffer zone of time during which they shed their working responsibilities. It's difficult for them to climb into their home life with any degree of eagerness when their job is still on their backs like a heavy load of bricks. (I think I understand why so many men stop off at a local bar for a beer or two before going home. It's their buffer zone between work and home, where they're expected to listen to more problems and conflicts with the wife and kids.)

Usually I just stand there in our bedroom and let Dick unwind at his own pace. Eventually he asks, "Well, what happened today that I should know about?" A word to wives at this point. Don't tell him anything but good news. The bills and broken-appliance news can wait until after he's had supper. Most men tend to be grumpy before they eat, so save the bad biggies for later. This time for dialogue is not fixed in length, but it is fixed on a daily basis. The channels of communication are at open-throttle position daily and any marriage needs this if it is to stay alive.

Another time we have for talking and listening is after the dinner hour. However, because of schedules this is not on a regular basis. That's probably why the time just after Dick gets home is so important to keeping our lives open to each other. There is one other time which is very special to us and that's Saturday morning at breakfast. It's our time to leisurely eat breakfast. As I've said before, Dick makes great pancakes and, even if the children are here, we take longer at this meal than any other because *we*

talk. When do you and your wife have a quick ten-minute
dialogue about the day's events? It really doesn't matter
when you have it, but that you do have it.

Second, is there any time in your week when you and
your wife can have a lunch, breakfast, or "whatever" together without the kids, friends, or relatives? A well-
known minister and his wife take one day a month to go
off together. They usually drive to the beach in the morning, take books to read, have lunch at a favorite restaurant
or have a small picnic, and then they spend the afternoon
walking, sharing, or just being quiet together. They have
four children, but one day a month just the husband and
the wife go away together. That day (only twelve days
each year) has held their marriage solidly together for
years, in spite of their crushing and hectic schedules.

At this point you may be saying, "Joyce, first of all I
don't have time at home to talk because I work eighteen
hours a day. Besides we don't have the money or the way
to spend a day at the beach like the minister you know."
I do understand about long hours and the unavailability
of time to talk, but you may have to decide which priority
is more important: making the money to support the family, or keeping a family together emotionally. The old
question from Matthew: ". . . what doth it profit a man if
he gains the whole world but loses his soul?" (*see* 16:26
KJV), is properly brought into focus here. You may have
to seriously reconsider which is truly more important to
you.

Many couples have to face the problems of making a
living and trying to hold their lives together. It is a very
scary, unreal time. I remember that time in our own lives.
My husband graduated in Business Administration and
was in retail selling for the first years of our marriage. The
only thing his job required of him was all of his waking
hours. When our marriage folded after five years, it didn't
take 20/20 vision to see where part of the blame rested.
After we became Christians, Dick took a detailed look at

the time the business consumed. It was then he began to seriously question whether the money and the job were all that important. The idea that he was in the wrong line of work grew stronger each day. We both began seeking God's direction as to what Dick should do and where he should start in regard to changing employment.

That was the very week he was fired! He was never fired before or since from any job, but it was God's rather dramatic way of getting my conscientious stick-it-out-no-matter-what husband to leave the wrong field.

Through a whole string of surprising events, beginning with Dick's being fired, God led us one step at a time into the right work. At thirty-five years of age Dick started at the bottom of the ladder in finance and the world of banking.

He had been in banking only a few years when our son, eighteen at the time, wrote a paper on family life and the generation gap for English class. Here is a part of what he wrote, titled "Generation Gap."

In my family there seems to be no generation gap. My parents are in their forties, my sister Laurie and I are both teenagers. But no problem of communication seems to exist between the two distinct age groups.

Ever since Laurie and I have been very young our parents took time from their work schedules and transformed it into family fun time. I can remember going to parks, to the show or to the beach. It was just the four of us together.

Dad and I joined the Boy Scouts and I have many fond memories of the adventures we experienced together.

Today my father is a banker. We don't see too much of him during the week. On the weekends, however, he spends his time with his family. He has a choice; he could play golf, go out with friends, sit and watch the boob tube, or be with us. Of these options he has wisely chosen the last.

My mother is exceptional and she holds a very special place in my heart. She doesn't pry into my world to see if she can help —but she's always there when I need her. We talk, share and exchange ideas. We are always learning about each other and what each of us believe.

My parents have given me the freedom of choice and I am now allowed to make my own decisions. In some instances they will suggest a particular course of action in a seemingly unsolvable problem, and trusting them fully I take their direction willingly.

We have a good rapport in our house—something that few families possess, and I thank God for it.

Rick's English teacher commented that he needed to develop each paragraph a little more, but he concluded the paper was good. It was also the only essay written in class which stated, ". . . there seems to be no generation gap."

I'm sure all the experiences and memories behind Rick's paper were due to Dick's efforts as a gut-level listener who was willing to make time for his family. Early in Rick's childhood Dick decided to *take time for his home life* and it has paid large dividends. Now that Rick and Laurie are married, those dividends are dear to us, for we are very close friends. I am grateful to God for that well-spent time Dick took with his children.

All of us are going to see our youngsters grow up and leave us to begin homes of their own; when that day comes I wonder what it will be like in your house. Will you sit across from your wife, drink your morning coffee, and read your paper without noticing or acknowledging old what's-her-name? Do you remember the coffee commercial that showed a man and woman at breakfast? At the table he read the paper and she read a book. He tasted the coffee and liked it, so he put down his paper and said, "It's really good." She lowered her book. He took a good look at her and said, "When did you get your nose fixed?" She gave him a funny stare and answered, "Two years ago. When did you grow bald?" He replied, "Eight years ago!" I always had a funny-sad reaction when I really listened to that commercial; there they were—living together—

yet they never saw or spoke to one another though they shared the same table, bed, and house.

That scene can happen to any of us if we have not been willing to listen, to share, and to communicate our true feelings. If you have not become friends with your wife during your thirties and forties, the age of retirement will come and it will be an unending, boring routine. You will have nothing to say to each other and no reason to listen to or to share your feelings.

It is up to you—in your house—to set the wheels of listening in motion. You may want to go over these seven areas with your wife.

1. Have you already stopped listening?
2. Do you listen without presuming or judging?
3. Do you ever listen by touching?
4. Are you communicating in honesty?
5. Do you communicate through written words?
6. Are you a gut-level listener?
7. Do you take time to listen?

At least if you ask her how she feels about this list and your abilities to communicate, you might see the beginning of something great!

My money is on you. I think you can be an exceptional listener, and your marriage can have exceptional communications!

SCRIPTURES

Communicating	Psalms 55:14
	Proverbs 12:12
	Proverbs 15:28
	Proverbs 18:13
	Romans 12:15
	James 1:19
	James 5:16
Listening to God	Proverbs 1:24–33
	Proverbs 2:1–15
	Proverbs 4:20–22

    About Talking   Proverbs 10:14
                              Proverbs 10:19–21
                              Proverbs 10:31, 32
                              Proverbs 10:12–14
                              Proverbs 12:26
                              Proverbs 15:4
                              Proverbs 18:4
                              Philippians 2:3, 4

RECOMMENDED READING

Narramore, Dr. Bruce. *Help! I'm a Parent.* Grand Rapids: Zondervan Publishing House, 1972.

Welch, Reuben. *We Really Do Need to Listen.* Nashville: Impact Books, 1978.

Wright, Norman. *Communication: Key to Your Marriage.* Glendale: Gospel Light, 1974.

6

The Wise Gentleman

> But the wisdom that comes from heaven is first of all
> pure and full of quiet gentleness. Then it is peace-
> loving and courteous. It allows discussion and is willing
> to yield to others; it is full of mercy and good deeds. It
> is wholehearted and straightforward and sincere.
>
> JAMES 3:17

Up to this point, I've been talking about what a woman
would like in her man, as far as the tough qualities are
concerned. Now, here are some tender traits.

"Why tender?" you ask. "Why not let the woman be in
charge of the tender department?" Because, dear man, if
you are tough without being tender, you run the risk of
being an iron-fisted tyrant. You could lose everything you
hold dear. On the other hand, should you be all tenderness, without the strength of toughness, you could become a weak sentimentalist.

What's really needed here is a godly balance: a toughness in your mind to resist sin and anything that corrupts
. . . tempered with a tender heart which reveals a pliable
and teachable spirit.

As much as I love my husband's consistently tough
qualities of character, I know if he does not balance them
off with tenderness—I will die. That sounds a bit dramatic
I know, but I'm the girl who lived in a marriage where all
was toughness and it drove me to a suicide attempt. My
spirit and possibly your wife's cannot survive in a marriage where: small courtesies are turned off; there are no
tender pats or back-of-the-neck kisses; or the humor is
heavy with sarcastic teasing and borders on insulting
rudeness. If it's true that the biggest problem in marriages

today is lack of open communication, then it's also true the missing ingredient in marriages is tenderness and the small acts of kindness which demonstrate your love.

Listed below are eleven words which have to do with being a wise gentleman. As you read them, try to remember incidences or conversations when you applied these words to your marriage. Mentally score yourself as to when these words became actions with your wife or children. It will be a great way to evaluate your *tender* abilities.

1. Consideration
2. Sympathy
3. Helpfulness
4. Tact
5. Courtesy
6. Compassion
7. Unselfishness
8. Politeness
9. Understanding
10. Thoughtfulness
11. Social manners

How did you rate? If you scored a perfect eleven points and could remember a recent time when you became each of those words in your daily life—you are definitely unreal. (Actually, you are a saint and best you get back to heaven where you belong.) If you scored about six or seven, I'd say you have a very special relationship going at your house and I'd guess your wife is deeply in love with you, and vice versa. If your score was three or less, there are probably some large gaps in your understanding of each other. I would guess also that your home, no matter how elegant or sparsely furnished, is a rather cold and uncomfortable place to live. By the way, if you scored either very high or very low, ask your wife to check the list. Get her evaluation of you and those words. She may knock off a few points or add some—you never know.

All of these tender qualities are important in a marriage (even though some of them overlap in areas) if your life together is to have a *wholeness* about it. Being tough without being tender just will not work for a *complete marriage*. The tender part of your character will be

closely tied in with *how you love*. Are you a lukewarm
lover, a passionate, romantic lover, a stale, old-shoe lover,
or what? At this point I'm not talking about sexual performance in the bedroom (I'll get to that later), but I'm
asking about the quality of your love in the kitchen or in
your family room.

If your loving is based on what you can get from your
wife, then you are in big trouble. You have married her
for all the wrong reasons. If her love for you is based on
the same selfish principle, she will quickly tire of you—
especially if you lose your job and the money runs out. You
will always remember her as "the little gold-digger who
took me for every dime I had." Your so-called love will not
hold up under the daily wear and tear of brushing your
teeth together, or the dull routines of working, eating,
and sleeping day after day. While you may stay with each
other for years, there will be nothing of love, gentleness,
or kindness between you.

On the other hand, if all through your loving comes the
thinking, the questioning, and the acting out of "What can
I *give* to you?"—you are on your way to a whale of a
marriage. In fact it is that kind of constant *giving love*
Paul is talking about in 1 Corinthians 13. The chapter is
commonly referred to as the Love Chapter of the Bible,
and we hear it frequently at weddings. Little do we know,
as we listen to those words at a wedding ceremony, what
it will really cost to love like that.

There is a letter on my desk right now from a tense
young woman who says, "How long must it be me who
gives all the time? I'm tired of giving and tired of his
taking, taking, taking." Unfortunately, real love is giving
all the time. I almost choked when I read Erich Segal's
now famous statement that love is never having to say
you're sorry, when in truth real love is exactly the opposite. Love is having to say "forgive me," and bona fide love
is giving forgiveness, taking apologies, and accepting the
other person unreservedly. Unimpeachable love is not

based on: "What's in it for me?" but rather "What can I do to make you happy?"

That giving kind of love is not unlike a fire in the fireplace. It will continue to burn only if new logs are supplied and old ashes are carried out. The gracious acts of sharing kindnesses and giving are the logs which are necessary to keep the love alive and growing. When we communicate our honest feelings and really hear each other, we are cleaning out the emotional ashes of our lives so the fire of love can burn unhindered.

I pray I am being practical, down-to-earth and crystal clear in this chapter. If you remember, one of the goals I set early in this book was the hope that you would fall madly and passionately in love with your wife. Here, then, are some ways for that to happen. I also believe these will help your wife, in turn, to share love with you. Anyway, I pray these things will help you both to learn how to *grow in love*. All of us, at one time in our lives, have fallen in love. (Remember your first love?) We have experienced that giddy euphoria, the detached-from-this-world sensation, but this love is different. This is all about growing (not merely falling) in love.

1. *Let her know you love her.* Some men I've talked with feel their actions speak for themselves. They say it is unnecessary to verbally say, "I love you." These same men list the material things they've given and they spell out their husbandly virtues. They rationalize that money and material things are evidence enough, and nothing more is needed. However, since your wife is made in a completely different way from you (you've noticed?), her emotional needs are totally different from yours also. We will always need those actions of yours, but they must be reinforced by verbal assurance. I personally think it's a small price to pay for a brightly lit fire.

Try calling your wife from work once in a while to say, "I was thinking of you and I love you!" You won't have time or opportunity to do this very often, but when you can, it is one of life's sweetest lifts for you both.

Remember to tell the Lord (in her presence) that you love her, but don't confine those beautiful words to just the Lord. Let others hear. Some of the most treasured times in my memory are when I've accidently overheard my husband tell someone about his love for me.

Occasionally tell her she's beautiful. She may not look anywhere near a Miss or Mrs. America, but she is beautiful —at least to you. When my husband has leaned over me and said, "Oh, I love those mouse-brown eyes of yours," (actually they are hazel brown flecked with green) he has *made me feel beautiful*. He's done that to me when I've been on my knees weeding the rose bed and dressed in my grubbiest, but it never fails to work. I feel beautiful.

You might suggest going out for a special dinner or just for hamburgers, but suggest it before she does. After you've worked all day at your job I know you want to stay at home, but in your wife's case, she may desperately need to be freed from making dinner and would really enjoy going out. This is a simple suggestion, but if it's been weeks since you've had dinner out with her, or been to the local pizza or hamburger joint, your wife is probably quite ready. If you ask her before she asks, she will *hear consideration and kindness* in your dinner plans, no matter what place you have in mind.

As I've said, she needs to hear you say the words *I love you*, but your actions must match your words. If they don't and you say, "Hon, I love you," be ready—she may come off very sarcastically with, "Oh, *sure* you do."

My friend Keith Korstjens said a long time ago the best advice he'd ever heard about growing in love was this instruction: Find a different way each day to say "I love you." Dick was standing by me when he heard Keith's statement, and I can honestly say that was the moment Dick pledged in his heart "to find a different way." He's been finding different ways ever since.

When he helps me with my coat he always manages to give me a secret little squeeze on my shoulders. Nobody ever sees the gesture because it's always done under my collar, but I am very aware of "I love you" with each squeeze. Many nights I have started to sit down for dinner and found on my chair a small, white bag from See's candy shop. It would be filled with thirty-two or fifty-nine cents' worth (or whatever change Dick had) of chocolate-covered almonds. I never see them being brought into the house, I just *find* them in various places. On one candy bag I saved Dick had written, "This is another way." I saved another white bag which originally held seventy cents' worth of Baklava, the Greek pastry; on it is written, "Just another way."

I know very few women who *expect* expensive gifts or dream of being given two dozen long-stemmed red roses. I do know of hundreds who are really turned on by a small bag of their favorite candy or an inexpensive bunch of spring flowers bought from the boy on the corner. To be given a tiny gift for no obvious reason and for no special occasion is mind-and-soul capturing. The wise man remembers that and practices it! Little things really do mean a lot to a woman, and if you find a different way to say "I love you" each day, it will say a thousand loving words for you.

Your wife will enjoy the little gifts of material things, but she needs the treasured gifts of your heart as well.

2. *Let her know you respect her.* We hear so much about having everything equal. Equal pay, equal rights, equal et cetera. Someone once asked me, "What is the best thing in your marriage, aside from knowing the Lord?" I remember thinking that through and then answering, *"Our equal and mutual respect* for each other." My response surprised me in one way because, why hadn't I said, "Our *love* is the best thing"—for it's really special. Instead, I'd used the words *equal respect.*

It occurs to me now that we lay too much of a burden on the overworked word *love*.

Show me a couple who respect each other, and I'll show you real love in action. Show me a couple who are in love, but where the two people do not respect each other, and I'll show you a very fragile relationship with the viable potential for fragmentation.

Everyone who knows Dick and me are truly aware that I have no head for business (It bores me silly), and that Dick is not terribly artistically creative.

Yet, you will never hear either one of us putting each other down for these traits. Why? Because we love each other? No. Because we respect each other's outside-the-home talents, parental skills, and personal abilities.

I am always a bit awestruck when I go into Dick's bank and observe his finely attuned aptitude to the whole world of banking. He's been in banking for years now, and I still marvel at God's leading and Dick's talent. In short, I respect this husband/father as I respect no other man I know.

By the same token, he has conveyed a hundred times to me that he simply does not know how I sit down in a room somewhere and pour myself out into writing a book, or stand before thousands of people and minister through verbal communication. Again, in short, he respects me.

Respect makes our love sparkle!

The husband of a dear friend of mine wrote me shortly after I'd visited with his wife. Read this excerpt from his letter and see the enormous respect he holds for her. Also notice that he is not in any way threatened by her talents or skills.

I again have to extend my appreciation for your time with my wife. She is a person who has a high level of ability and sensitivity. She is often frustrated by low challenges and low interpersonal involvement. Your time with her always seems to "recharge her tanks." She has big dreams and big goals and there are not many people around who encourage that or even can understand it. Her time with you seems to confirm the Lord's direction in her life as she continues to press on. It excites and thrills me to see her meet these challenges and continue to grow in Jesus. I am so humbly thankful to our Lord Jesus for the relationship that He has given to us. *We are so different in many ways* and yet we have been convinced from the very moment of meeting almost that God has put us together for very special reasons. I appreciate your involvement in encouraging us to continue to believe in those *special reasons.*

Respect not only makes love sparkle, it gives a marriage the enduring quality so necessary to continued commitment.

3. *Invest in your wife's stock in front of your children.* It's a scary but true thing; our children watch us, their parents, like young, hungry hawks looking for edible prey. They never miss a thing. Each wink, look, or critical comment which passes between parents is duly noted and stored in their little computerlike minds.

Just reach over, pat your wife's hand (or whatever) and say ever so quietly, "Hi, Honey, how did it go today?" and all the little people's eyes, minds, and ears take it in. (In our house, even the dog gets into the act because with Dick's first attentive pat on me, the dog virtually goes bananas.) Since our children do watch and study us so very much, it is a marvelous thing when either the husband or the wife invests in the other's stock for the children to store in their memory banks. Some children's memories are filled with arguments, some with silence, some with deep-seated hatred, but all children will retain their memories. It's my belief that we should do everything in our power to try to be the kind of people who produce positive, heartwarming recollections and memories for our children.

My stock has gone up considerably during these years of family life and Dick has endeared himself to me every time he's taken the time to do it. Once at dinner, just as we held hands for our dinner prayer, Dick said, "Rick and Laurie, if you both marry someone who is half the person your mother is, you will be very blessed." Mothers store memories, too, and now that Rick is married to Teresa I often remember Dick's words. I especially remember them when someone says, "Teresa is so much like you, Joyce."

I remember the time when I went to Dick and said, "I've had an awful day with Laurie. She is mad at her school, her teachers, and her mother, so today has been quite a hassle. Can you help invest in my stock tonight?" All day I'd felt I'd lost both the battle and the war.

Later, at one point in the evening I heard Dick say, "Laurie, I really like that dress you're wearing. Where did you get it?"

After she told him what he already knew ("Mother made it.") he said, "Great! Isn't it neat that your mother is so creative? That dress would cost a fortune if we had to buy it, but that mom of yours can really sew."

I saw my stock rise a few points, and I listened as Laurie said slowly, "Yeah—that's right. We did see one like this the other day and it cost $30, but Mom made this for $6.50." Of course that was years ago when *nothing* cost like it does today!

Another way to invest in your wife's stock is to show her you care about helping around the house. Your job may keep you tied up eighteen hours a day, you may be exhausted by the time you reach your house, but even helping a little says volumes about your tenderness. Straightening up the living room, taking out the trash, or using cleanser on the bathroom sink may take one and one-half to three minutes of your time, but your entire family will notice. To your wife it says, "I love you." To your children it says, "He cares."

Helping your wife is essential if she holds an outside-the-home job or if you have children under ten at your house. She can always use the help. If a man has ever had to fill in as a full-time housekeeper and mother to his children because his wife was sick or away, he always comes out of it a changed man! After the experience, no matter how brief, he never says or even implies, "This being a housewife is a snap!" Nor does he ever come home from work again, look around and say, "What have you done today with all that free time?"

Children are quick to see if Daddy pitches in to help. I've also found it was much easier to get my children to clean up their rooms and hang up their clothes when we all shared the work load. Each family is different in size and schedules, but helping each other out with the work load frees the entire family for playtime.

Investing in your wife's stock pays long-lasting dividends not only in the memories of your children, but in the heart of your wife's memories as well.

4. *Cultivate and maintain a sense of humor.*   Of all the creative things God made, like flowers, animals, oceans, and deserts, the only thing capable of laughter is mankind. No flower can chuckle, no horse can giggle, and no mountain can throw its head back and laugh—only people can. God meant for us to use our vocal ability to laugh, yet when we do it, we generally do it sparingly and sometimes with guilt.

"The pressures of life, Joyce," you say, "are too horrible to go around laughing. Too many people are hurting and dying for us to be having a funny fit of the ha-ha's." You're right and certainly I am not unaware of world conditions or the sadness which hangs like a doomsday cloud above us, but this is a plea for us to gain our balance in regard to humor.

Having a good sense of humor does not mean telling jokes, one after the other, like George Jessel at some

banquet. It does not mean meeting the end of someone's
sentences with a one-liner that breaks everybody up. It
simply means never taking yourself too seriously. It
means being able to look at a crummy situation as it happens and realize that, while you may not like it or understand it, it probably won't start a third world war.

People without a sense of humor generally act and
speak as if they live at the city morgue. They miss the
important fact that God gave us the gift of humor and
laughter because He knew how well it would heal our
ravaged souls. He knew in these fragile days we need
humor more than at any time.

After Bob Hawkins published my cookbook, *Mix Butter with Love,* he and his wife, Shirley, invited us over
for a dinner at their house. I remember the evening as
delightful; but one of the highlights of that time was
being enchanted by a most captivating original drawing
by the late Richard Hook. I'll never forget my first look
at it for it simply astonished me. It is a picture of Jesus
(as only Richard Hook could draw) flanked on either side
by two of His disciples. They have just returned from
fishing, the boat behind them is probably on Lake Gali-
lee, and all three are wading toward the shore. The most
completely captivating thing about the picture is the
fact that all of them have their arms around each other's
shoulders, their heads are thrown back and all three are
joyously laughing. I thought, "What an incredible, marvelous thing—they are laughing with God. How good
that must have felt, and how soothed their souls must
have been that day."

We need to laugh within our families and with others.
Ask yourself these two questions: Are you fun to live with?
and Would you like to be married to you? This will give
you a pretty good idea whether or not you are taking life
too seriously, or if humor is an effortless thing at your
house.

Try using humor in a creative way. My husband's

humor is quiet and dry, but always in motion. Once when I had neglected the dusting in our house just long enough to drive his Mr. Neat complex up the nearest wall, he wrote with his finger on the piano lid, "Joyce, please dust me. I need it."

Another time he was trying to get me to hang up a number of my clothes in our bedroom. In delightful humor he laid out my clothes on our bed and made it look like someone was lying there. He had placed one of my wigs on my pillow, then below that there was a necklace, a sweater, skirt, my hose, and finally my shoes. It all looked as if I'd just evaporated from this world. It worked, and when I stopped laughing, I put every last thing away. (That day at least.) Creative humor in our homes can take a lot of sting out of daily living.

Dick and I have a few friends we only see on rare occasions, and that's good, because being with them means laughing. One evening of being together and our stomach muscles are shot for two weeks from talking and laughing together. We infect each other from the moment we see one another until we go our separate ways. When we are with them we stay just barely on the sane edge of hysteria. Do you know anybody like that? Someone with whom you can share your biggest disappointment one minute, and two minutes later you start making smart remarks, or puns, or plays on words, and end up laughing? I do, and any time I'm with them my heart has experienced a healing only laughter can bring.

One word of caution about humor. Our country is overrun with humor loaded with sarcasm and criticism. That kind of humor is highly damaging to the soul. Teasing humor may be funny to you but, because it attacks the other person's feeling of self-worth, is annihilating to that person. Check yourself to see whether you have to punctuate your sentences with, "I'm just kidding," or, "I didn't mean that." If those sentences come up regularly in your

conversations, you are probably not being funny and your
humor needs an overhauling. Also you are probably not
communicating what you really do mean.

We must be sure we are laughing with our loved ones
and not at them, for it is the difference between wound-
ing or healing. Maintaining a sense of humor between
husband and wife can be a great adventure. Just how
great an adventure was written down on paper by Bob
Benson in his small, but delightful, book *Laughter In The
Walls.* Here is the title piece.

Laughter In The Walls

I pass a lot of houses on my way home—
   some pretty,
     some expensive,
     some inviting—
but my heart always skips a beat
   when I turn down the road
and see my house nestled against the hill.
   I guess I'm especially proud
of the house and the way it looks because
   I drew the plans myself.
It started out large enough for us—
   I even had a study—
two teenaged boys now reside in there.
   And it had a guest room—
my girl and nine dolls are permanent guests.
   It had a small room Peg
had hoped would be her sewing room—
   the two boys swinging on the dutch door
have claimed this room as their own.
   So it really doesn't look right now
as if I'm much of an architect.
   But it will get larger again—
one by one they will go away
   to work,
     to college,
     to service,
   to their own houses,
and then there will be room—

a guest room,
   a study,
and sewing room
for just the two of us.
But it won't be empty—
   every corner
      every room
   every nick
      in the coffee table
will be crowded with memories.
Memories of picnics,
   parties, Christmases,
   bedside vigils, summers,
      fires, winters, going barefoot,
   leaving for vacation, cats
      conversations, black eyes
   graduations, first dates,
      ball games, arguments
   washing dishes, bicycles
      dogs, boat rides
   getting home from vacation
      meals, rabbits and
a thousand other things
   that fill the lives
of those who would raise five.
And Peg and I will sit
quietly by the fire
   and listen to the
   laughter in the walls.

When the children are gone, no lunches are to be made,
and retirement sets in—what will you hear in your walls?
I pray it's laughter, for God created laughter as well as
tears for our lives.

5. *Take a good look at the social manners in your life and
home.* There seems to be some confusion as to what
exactly manners are or are not. I've collected what I've
learned from men in my seminars as to what they believe
manners are all about.

Manners Are Not	*Manners Are*
1. Sissy, unmasculine, and quite unnecessary with today's independent liberated woman.	1. The highest form of Christ-like love. What Paul meant when he said a husband should love his wife as Christ loved the church.
2. Trying to be something you are not. Being uppity as Mrs. Astor's horse. Having a smooth, oily, and completely false personality which is not you.	2. Often small, but honest and real, acts of kindness. Done because you honor one another, and besides, you are the prince—she the princess!
3. Formal and unflexible, a rigid set of rules which close in on your home, making it a prison—not a haven.	3. The most gracious way to build memories for your wife and children.

I will never forget a student from our tenth-grade Sunday school class who came to our house for dinner one Sunday. After dinner he quietly cornered me in my kitchen and confidentially asked, "Does Dick always treat you that way—even when you two are alone?"

"Treat me what way?" I whispered back.

He said, "You know—*nice.*"

When I assured him that Dick wasn't putting on an act for company I asked, "Why did you ask such a question?"

His answer still stings my soul. (Both of his parents were active, involved Christians at our church.) He said, "I have never seen my father do one single act of kindness for my mother. I've never seen him open a car door or seat her at dinner; what's more, I don't ever remember either my mom or my dad saying anything kind to each other in front of me."

I believe strongly that manners are not some set of rigid rules laid down by Emily Post or Amy Vanderbilt, but rather they are acts of kindness. The young boy in my kitchen was not aware of the technical rules of good eti-

quette, but he had sensed the tenderness that passed between a man and a woman at dinner.

I also believe manners are sorely missing from many
Christian homes. I remember during my childhood in the
1930s and 40s there was a general disdain for anything
that smacked of etiquette. It was as if etiquette was a
nine-letter, dirty word. It's only a guess of mine, but to me
the emphasis and teaching of the church on daily living
seemed to be aimed only at Bible study and prayer
groups. While I agree wholeheartedly with that, it left
little or no time for teaching kindness. No one preached
sermons on a husband and wife being tenderhearted and
kind to one another as Ephesians 4:32 proclaimed. In fact,
if you had manners or had the reputation of being a gentleman, you were accused of putting on airs, trying to be
something you weren't, or (worse) you were not tending
to spiritual matters.

I've always been struck by the cultural differences in
manners between Christian and non-Christian men. The
Christian men have usually been outclassed by the non-
Christian men. My first chance to see the difference between Christian and non-Christian homes came when I
was about eight. We were living in Canada and I was
invited to dinner at the home of one of my school friends.
My parents discussed the whole thing rather like it was a
decision involving shipping ammunition to a new war.

When I questioned what all the fuss was about, I remember my mother saying, "Well, Betty's parents are not
Christians. They are very wealthy and Betty's father is an
avowed atheist." (Even at eight I knew "atheist" was bad!)
She continued, "Dad and I don't want you to be in that
kind of home."

In the end they agreed that after all it was only an
invitation to dinner, so I went. I can tell you I was certainly not properly prepared for the whole evening. It
was definitely the opposite of anything I'd anticipated.

The maid announced dinner with a beautiful crystal

bell. The father had just barely come home from work, but he warmed the whole dining room with his smile. He slipped up behind his wife, hugged her, pulled out her chair, and seated her. I'd never seen both those things done together just before a meal. He then kissed his daughter's head, smiled at me and said, "Now, who do we have here?" After he chatted with me a second, he seated both of us, and then took his chair at the head of the long table.

The flowers and candlelight were beautiful—the food delicious; but what I remember the most was that the laughter, the sharing, and the tremendous love which flowed around the family and the maid, swept even to me —the young, wide-eyed stranger in their midst.

Later my mother asked, "Was it just awful?"

"Oh, Mother," I bubbled. "No, it was the most wonderful night of my life!"

For a long time I described each little detail and the beauty of it all. Now that I look back on that dinner, I can see that the maid, the decor, and the flowers were just smashing; but the most impressive memory that lingers is the overwhelming *kindness I saw being practiced* in that home. Their manners came as easy as their love, and I couldn't help but compare them with so many tension-filled homes we'd been invited to. Those homes, even though they were Christian homes, had families and dinners that never knew a joyous loving time of living. That night was the first night I'd ever seen a bona fide gentleman in action. I was impressed all right! Even then I didn't understand why Christians, who were supposed to be filled with love toward each other, did not have a wonderful time together at dinner like the people in my friend's home did.

After our daughter had been dating a couple of years, she flopped down on the couch next to me and said, "Oh, Mom, I'm so discouraged about boys. Christian boys have no manners at all! When I get married I want to marry a

man like Dad or Rick because I like the way they treat you
—but I don't think there are any left like that!"

A few weeks later she dated a boy from our church. He
was a Christian, but his parents were not. He had been
reared with all the special social manners you could ac-
quire. Our whole family was delighted with a remark he
made as he was opening the car door one night for Laurie.
He said, "Tell your mother I'm so glad she raised you with
manners. You don't know how many girls won't wait for
me to open the door. I guess most Christian girls don't
have manners anymore."

The young are not the only ones who see the need for
tender acts of kindness. A minister I know made his own
survey of the men in his church and their manners. After
every Sunday morning service for one month, he raced
up to a second-story window which overlooked the
church parking lot. There he observed the families of his
congregation as they left the church. His survey revealed
that three out of four husbands acted out this poor scene
of togetherness each Sunday. The husband reached the
car first. Sometimes he honked the horn impatiently. Finally his wife would appear carrying the baby, and sometimes two small ones were clinging to her and the diaper
bag. She couldn't get into the car until he unlocked it from
inside. Usually while she was trying to get the small children into the backseat, the baby's bottle or some other
object would drop. The pastor could tell there was some
unpleasant dialogue going on during this time. He found
out later it usually concerned (1) how long it took the wife
to get out to the car, and (2) how much of the football
game the husband had already missed. Only one husband
out of four helped his wife to get into the car. Only one
out of four showed concern for getting his family home.

A man I've known for some years never opened the car
door for his wife or any other woman. He felt it was a sissy
Emily Post kind of thing to do and, "Besides," he was fond
of saying, "she doesn't have two broken arms." His table

manners left much to be desired, and manners in general
were looked upon by him as quite unnecessary.

After many years of marriage, the wife died and her
husband was heartbroken because he truly loved her.
Somehow, as the pallbearers brought her casket out of the
funeral service, the husband and his family reached the
hearse ahead of them. The mortician was back a few feet
and, since he knew the husband quite well, he called him
by name and said, "Open the door for her, will you?" The
man reached for the door handle and then, for one second, just froze. He realized he had never opened a car
door for her in life; now in her death it would be the first,
last, and only time. It was a moment for him when years
of regrets came crushing down around him.

We all have our reasons for not practicing kindness or
for withholding small courtesies, but they don't hold up
too well after our loved one is gone.

I think this chapter on the wise gentleman is important
to me because in the New Testament I see the theme of
kindness strongly presented. God's love and forgiveness
seems to be the number one message of the New Testament. However, running a close second is this business of
being kind, of showing gentleness, and of having the spirit
of consideration for each other. Evidently the Lord
thought it was very important to not only love each other,
"A new commandment I give unto you, That ye love one
another; as I have loved you . . ." (John 13:34 KJV), but to
be *kind* as well. We hear phrases like: "in honour prefer-
ring one another" (*see* Romans 12:9 KJV); and be kind and
tender-hearted toward one another (*see* Ephesians 4:32
KJV). These and other verses indicate how much God is
concerned with our *tender* abilities. That is why, earlier
in the chapter, I said that manners are the highest form
of Christ-like love. Read the verse in Galatians 5 which
says, "but the fruit of the spirit is love, joy, peace, patience, kindness, goodness, faithfulness, gentleness, and
self-control" (*see* 5:22). I can never read it without thinking that God's plan for us is to live these words, practice

them, and most important of all, to *be these words* in private and in public.

My speaking and singing has taken me into hundreds of banquets, luncheons, seminars, and just plain old meetings. While some of those engagements were for non-churched people, most of them were involved with some kind of Christian function. (Even my military tours have all been for the U.S. Chaplain Corps.) I've eaten at enough church banquets to say that from the manners I've seen I can only conclude that many Christian households do not practice even the basics of social manners. Here are a few typical examples.

Across the table (if I'm not at a head table) sits a fifteen-year-old girl chewing with her mouth open and sloshing her food around like clothes in an open washing machine. I don't have far to look to see how she got that way.

Next to her is her mother who looks like the same washing machine, only she's the eighteen-pound-load model.

Next to them sits a man hunched over his plate with both arms firmly fixed onto the table. He's in a different world as he slides the food off his plate, catching it in his mouth.

Another woman wolfs her food down "fastest and firstest." Trying to get her to pass the salt, or say hello, is just not possible.

The man next to her is a speed-eater too. After he's had two desserts (the rest of us are still on the salad), he shoves his chair back and blesses us with a hearty belch. When he notices that a few ladies' backs have stiffened with the rumble of his belch, he reminds everyone of the old Arab custom (or is it African?) of belching to show you liked the dinner. Ho. Ho.

Am I being too hard on these people? I doubt it, because I'm not sharing some of the really gross things I've seen at church banquets. The sad part is this: If people have such terribly poor manners in public places like churches and restaurants, you can bet at home it's 100 percent worse.

Our daughter, Laurie, has worked on and off as a waitress ever since she has been seventeen. She even spent
one hard but glorious summer waitressing at Hume Lake
Christian Conference Center. But when she's employed
in a secular restaurant, she frankly agrees with other wait-
resses that Sunday is the worst day to work. As one of her
non-Christian waitress friends said, "It's horrible on Sundays with all those Christians [she pronounces the word
like it's a disease] coming in. All you hear is griping and
unreasonable demands from them. They have little fights
among themselves, they complain about the menu and
the prices, and they are just plain disagreeable. Then,
after I serve their food, they stop everything, bow their
heads, fold their hands, and pray their little prayer. It
blows my mind because right after the prayer they are
their same mean old selves."

Once, when a waitress pointed out a family that had
really hassled her, Laurie was horrified to see it was a local
church youth pastor and his wife.

We are all held accountable for the looks on our faces,
for our conduct, for our talk, and yes, even for our actions,
manners, and treatment of others. My daughter has had
quite a difficult time witnessing to that waitress because
many of God's children don't act as if they are.

I'm suggesting that, if we say we are a real born-again
child of God, we need to examine our attitudes and our
manners and work out some kindness goals which may be
missing. We hear and read much about giving out the
Good News of Christ and of being a witness. We tend to
think that witnessing means knocking on doors and sharing the plan of salvation; but let me tell you—we are
never so loud a witness as when (publicly or privately) we
are unkind to each other or those around us.

Let me write a few words about the dinner hour in our
homes. When I wrote the cookbook *Mix Butter With Love*
it was really a love letter to my daughter-in-love, Teresa.
Since you probably will never get around to reading a
cookbook, I want to share part of the last chapter. I wrote:

A famous psychiatrist once said, "Tell me in detail what your evening dinner hour is like and I'll tell you about your family relationships." That should give you a fair idea of how important the dinner hour is.

We tend to think that everyone's dinner time is just like the one we are accustomed to. If we have had lots of infighting and bickering at the table, we think that's normal. If we have had meat, potatoes, and no vegetables or salads, we think that's the only way to eat. If we've had a centerpiece of flowers and candles every dinner hour, we think that's the way it is with all families' dinner hour.

But in talking with many people and teaching a creative cooking class to Azusa Pacific College students I've learned a whole lot about dinner hours.

In the first place, *everyone* has a different experience to share. Whenever I've asked if the memory of eating together in their home was a happy or a painful one, I've been astounded with the answers. Nine out of ten said it was rather painful. Here are some examples: Some families never have a time when they all sit together for one meal (dinner, lunch, or breakfast). Some gather silently, gulp all food down as fast as possible, and without conversation, disappear with the last mouthful. Still others collect at the end of the day to have dinner and one long fight. Many families have highly *un*balanced meals (all starchy foods or meat and potatoes with no vegetables or greens of any kind). Some families use the dinner hour to discuss (critically) people and problems. *Rare* is the family who comes to the dinner table hungry for food and fellowship and leaves richly satisfied in both areas.

This last dinner hour is what I would pray for you to have. It won't be easy; and will require a meeting of minds between you and your husband. It will take time and effort on your part, but you are about to build a tower of memories and at this point in your life you can decide whether those memories will be happy or painful.

When I talked about the responsibility of setting a pleasant, warm table, I wrote:

Setting a pleasant, warm table begins by bringing your family *around* a table. Then use placemats for everyday and table-

cloths for special times. Finally, complete the table picture by
using a centerpiece of flowers, fruit, or some fun decoration and
candles.

The first time I made a centerpiece of three or four flowers
from our yard and lit two candles at dinner time I took quite
a ribbing. I'll never forget it!

First, my husband made all kinds of cracks like, "Why is it so
dark in here? Is the food so bad that we are trying to cover it
up?" Then both he and our son decided maybe the food *did*
look better that night by candlelight. Later, while I was having
a fun fit, they got hysterical with laughter as they decided not
only did the food definitely look better by candlelight, but I did,
too!

Long after dinner that night, and in the privacy of our bedroom, I talked with my husband. I told him how much fun
dinner had been, but that I *was serious* about flowers and candlelight. I felt it was our only time to be together as a family.
It was our only time to talk to each other, to find out how it was
going in everyone's world and to share a bit of ourselves with
each other. I wanted it to be a happy, warm time and I asked
my husband if he would share the responsibility with me in
making great memories for us and our children. I think, at that
point, he didn't think flowers and candlelight made *that* much
difference, but he was a great sport and said he'd back me all
the way. (*Bless* him!!)

Quite often when someone stops by during our dinner they
always see our table, and say, "Oh, I'm sorry, I didn't know you
were having a special party tonight." My husband always beams
with that special smile of his and says, "No, no special party.
This is standard procedure for every dinner hour at our house."
It's a beautiful time for all of us and our hearts will always hold
these treasured memories.

Some years ago, I was teaching two seminars on Family
Fun and Fellowship at a Sunday School Convention. During the first seminar I told about the need for manners, for
candlelight and flowers, and for acts of kindness at our
dinner tables. At the first session a darling couple came
up, and the husband good-naturedly said, "Well, I'm a

knife-licker at the table—have been all my life and don't think I'm going to change now." We all laughed until his wife said, rather seriously, that she really didn't like their dinner hour; furthermore she added, their boys "were beginning to take after their father." Now, before you say, "What's so big about knife-licking? After all, if he wants to do it—let him!" let me finish my story. This may not be a problem in your life, but it was in theirs.

The next session came. Afterwards Ted (the knife-licker) and his wife told me of their week. Ted had gone out into their yard, picked some flowers, brought them in to his wife and said, "I'd like you to arrange these for our table and I'd like candlelight, too." She arranged the flowers and began to fix dinner. It was the first time in her memory that she could remember being excited about cooking, and by the time dinner came she was sincerely enjoying it. They had fun at their table. Their conversations got their sons to share what they'd done that day. It was the warmest family time they'd ever had around their table. Somewhere in the middle of dinner, the wife was very surprised to hear her husband make this little speech.

It went something like this. "Boys, you know I'm a knife-licker, but I don't think it's very good manners, and besides it upsets your mother terribly, so I'm not going to lick my knife at the table anymore. Sometimes on Saturday when I'm fixing my own lunch I will lick my knife, but I'm not going to do it at the table—and neither will either of you. We are going to have a beautiful table with good food and fun talk from now on."

I've chosen to use this illustration in preference to many others I have heard because it was so small a thing, yet so big an issue at their home. I've talked with them on two occasions since the seminars and their dinner hour has become what they hoped it would be. However, they were willing to take a good look at their manners and do something about them. Ted's decision will have its impact on his sons—not to mention his wife—for years to come.

During our children's teen years, I alternated between them and I took either Rick or Laurie with me to out-of-town engagements. Once when Rick was fifteen, we flew to San Diego for an afternoon radio show and a Christmas banquet at a church that evening. Later that night we arrived back at the airport only to find all planes grounded by heavy fog. We stayed overnight and went to the airport early the next morning. Since we had an hour-and-a-half wait for a plane, we decided to have breakfast in the airport's restaurant. I'll never forget that special time. Before I could say anything to the hostess, my son quickly stepped ahead of me and said, "Our name is Landorf—party of two." As we reached our table, he seated me. I remember blinking a bit in surprise and feeling ridiculously pleased.

We sat down and chatted about whether we were hungry or not (he was, I wasn't) and casually talked of what we'd eat. I was just about to order when our son looked up at the waitress and said, "She would like a warm Danish roll, small orange juice, and coffee. I'd like number three on the breakfast menu and no coffee."

It was a little too much. I could hardly believe this was the typical teenager I'd lived with for fifteen years—he had changed so before my eyes!

"Rick," I began. "I am very impressed with your manners and your polite way of handling the hostess, the waitress, and me. Frankly, though, I don't remember anyone sitting you down and teaching you these things one by one—so who did?"

He casually said, "No one has taught me, Mom, I've just been watching Dad for years." His answer kept me silent and thinking for a long time because I hadn't realized we were being watched and studied as models.

In his last Mother's Day letter to me before he married Teresa, he wrote in part:

Mom,

This is my last Mother's Day at home. This summer you will be sending out the first of your two "projects" to build a house of his own. I'm not leaving under duress, or just "to get out" but I am standing firm on my own two feet proud of where I came from.

For the last twenty years you have been shaping, molding and even cultivating me as your son.

I have watched your marriage succeed. I have *seen* the unseeable love between you and Dad. I have felt God bring our family together as one unit.

We had no idea he was watching us so closely, but he had observed us for all his brief twenty years. Your children are watching, learning, and soaking in your actions as a dad, too.

When the great journalist Stewart Alsop died of cancer, much was written and said of him in eulogies, but one paragraph in a *Newsweek* editorial captured my heart. It said:

Stew rarely raised his voice or lowered his guard in public. He was respectful of his elders, gracious with his colleagues, considerate of children, loyal to friends, and at all times manifested a pre-liberation attitude of courtesy toward women. Even when his body was corroded with pain, Stew would struggle to his feet when a woman entered the room. (June 3, 1974)

His "attitude of courtesy" was alive and well, even while he was in the acute pain of dying, and my admiration of his tender qualities knows no limits.

When I spoke to the male students of Biola College on *Tough and Tender*, many young men made the identical comment regarding my remarks. In the weeks to follow, I received dozens of letters and they repeated the same thought:

Mrs. Landorf, until you spoke at Chapel no one had ever confronted me with all the reasons and aspects of why I should be a Christian gentleman. No one ever spoke to my heart about my need to be courteous or to be the wise Christian gentleman God wants me to be. Thank you. I shall be a better man for today's chapel service.

For them to be the *better man* will not be an easy task. Balancing between *tough and tender* on the see-saw of life demands daily guidance from the Lord, but that guidance *is* available. However, it gets back to our ability to love—for if our love is the giving kind, then our actions will speak for themselves.

The following is not a quiz but merely a "manners" checklist. Remember, having manners simply means being kind to one another.

1. What is the dinner hour like at your house?
2. How long has it been since you told your wife she looked nice, cooked your favorite dish, or that you were proud of her?
3. Have you ever written your wife a note and told her three things you like about her?
4. Are you and your wife setting the right example for your children in regard to kindness in the home?
5. Do you have an equal respect for each other?
6. Are you fun to live with?
7. How do you think others will remember you, after you're gone?

I read once, and I can't remember where, that the very best portion of a good man's life was found in his little, nameless, unremembered acts of kindness and of love. I agree, and I must add that courtesy (as represented by those little, nameless, unremembered acts of kindness) is the oil and lubricant for all relationships—but especially as used by the wise gentleman.

SCRIPTURES

Gentleness   Psalms 18:35
                                    1 Corinthians 4:18–21
                                    Galatians 5:22, 23
                                    Ephesians 4:2
                                    1 Thessalonians 2:7
                                    1 Timothy 6:11
                                    2 Timothy 2:24
                                    Titus 3:2
                                    1 Peter 2:18
                                    1 Peter 3:4

Biblical definition
  of a wise gentleman   James 3:17
Jesus described Himself   Matthew 11:29, 30
Paul describes Jesus'
  gentleness   2 Corinthians 10:1
The giving kind of love   1 Corinthians 13

RECOMMENDED READING

Benson, Bob. *Laughter In The Walls.* Nashville: Impact Books, 1969.

Shedd, Charlie. *Promises to Peter.* Waco: Word, Inc., 1970.

Vanauken, Sheldon. *A Severe Mercy.* London: Hodder & Stoughton 1977.

7

The Gentle Lover

> But remember that in God's plan men and women
> need each other. For although the first woman came
> out of man, all men have been born from women ever
> since, and both men and women come from God their
> Creator.
>
> 1 CORINTHIANS 11:11, 12

As far as sex goes at our house, we have always had this
little saying, "Loving starts in the kitchen." Now, I realize
this might not sound too profound. Or does it? Maybe,
from your masculine reasoning, loving or being a lover
has nothing whatsoever to do with the kitchen. However,
that's not quite the way it is with women.

We are incurable romanticists and our taste for romance never dies, tires, or gets old. Most women do not,
I repeat, do not long to be romanced in the style befitting
an Italian princess or an English queen. We do not pine
away the hours in endless fantasies about dinner for two
on the Riviera surrounded by flowers and strolling vio-
linists. We are much more realistic than that. But we need
romance in our lives, and we'd settle for a lot less than
dinner on the Riviera.

Little things, like a slight (but definite) sexy wink from
you across a crowded room, can do wonders for us!

When my grandparents were in their seventies, they
were deeply in love and Grandpa was still a lover. I can
remember time and time again seeing my grandfather
enter a room which was bursting with family (like on
Christmas Day) and watching him as he looked for
Grandma. When his eyes found her, his face would light
up like sunshine and he would wink at her. We never

were able to find out what exactly that wink meant, but to this day we still talk about how Grandma used to blush beet-red when he did it.

Our toes would curl up in our shoes over you, if you slipped up behind us at the kitchen stove and kissed the back of our neck. A man in one of my seminars laughed out loud when I suggested kissing his wife's neck and said, "The one place I can never kiss my wife is on her super ticklish neck. She'd kill me if I did that!" So I suggested a couple of other areas I felt would be safer, yet do the job.

We women would be delighted beyond description to watch you walk through the front door and see reflected on your face the thought: "I'm glad I'm home because you are here." These in-the-kitchen romances are vitally needed for a zestful sexuality between a husband and wife. Many couples in marriage have skipped the whole concept of loving starting in the kitchen. They have limited their loving habits and practices to the bedroom area of their house only. It's no wonder the wife feels she's being used by an oversexed husband, and the husband feels he's been neglected by a frigid wife. You can be highly skilled and/or educated in sexual techniques but still be a lousy lover—especially if you ignore the loving-starting-in-the-kitchen policy.

From the romantic viewpoint of a woman, she feels she needs gentle loving in the kitchen, continued through dinner and the rest of the evening, or you can forget about sex by bedtime. (I don't care what the manual says about changing her mind in bed.) Making love and having sexual intercourse may happen in your bedroom; but unless the seeds of romance and gentle love are planted in the kitchen, it may be an experience in frustration.

A young minister who was honestly trying to practice the principle of loving starting in the kitchen shared his inner heart with me when he said, "My wife and I get along very well, but we have one serious area of conflict in our lives. It seems every time we sit down to eat our

evening meal, the phone rings, and it's always for me. My
wife wants me to ignore it and let it ring, but I'm a minister and I feel guilty if I don't answer it. Almost every night
we argue over this, and of course, it spoils our dinner time
with our family and each other. But I'm caught in the
middle of a difficult dilemma. I'm torn between my responsibility to my church, on one hand, and my love for
my family on the other. Tell me, should I—dare I—let it
ring?"

I didn't have to ask him how his love life was surviving
(though I now wish I had), but I did have a fair idea. Based
on what I know about women, I'd guess that his wife's
heart would not be sufficiently healed by bedtime from
the wounds she got during the dinner hour. In a typical
woman's logic, I knew she'd reason, "If he really loved
me, he would let that blasted phone ring. But he seems
to love his church more. He doesn't think enough of me
to talk to me, so I guess I'm only needed when we go to
bed."

Sexual intercourse preceded by this kind of emotional
battle is certainly possible and even probable, but it
comes nowhere near to being the delightful, congenial
experience God intended. Going to bed with a woman
who suggests you love someone (or something) more than
her can be downright uncomfortable. It's going to be
pretty icy between those sheets no matter how high
you've turned up the electric blanket.

I asked the Lord to give me an illustration for this young
pastor because I loved his concern and his genuine desire
to do the right thing. I hoped He would give me something practical and workable, because this problem with
the phone is a very familiar one in everyone's life-style
today.

Alexander Graham Bell did our whole world a fantastic
service when he invented the telephone. The phone has
now become a real necessity of life, but the longer I live
with phones, the more I wonder if we aren't paying an
unreasonable amount of attention to their ringing. House-

wives drop everything from the laundry to (sometimes) the baby in order to answer a phone's urgency. If you are a businessman you know you can call on a man in his office and, just as you are getting into your business, his phone rings. Of course he answers it. You can twiddle your thumbs for any length of time while he chats. Frustration sets in quickly because this was your allotted, prearranged time to talk, and yet—there you sit.

The minister was right in his concern about his phone calls. Many people are just now beginning to evaluate and measure the extent to which a ringing phone will dictate their life-styles. "Tell me," I asked him, "when a surgeon is in the middle of performing surgery, do they ever ask him to leave his patient and answer an outside phone call?"

"No, probably not," he answered.

"Right," I agreed. "Now, tell me why." And I waited for his answer.

Very thoughtfully he said, "Well, I guess it's because his patient and his surgery are too important to be interrupted."

"Exactly!" I said, and he got the message loud and clear.

When this man lets his phone ring during the time it takes to eat dinner, he is saying in the most romantic, loving way possible, "My dear wife and family, you are very important to me. You are all valuable to me and for the next brief moments you are going to have my undistracted attention. No phone, no TV blaring, and no one coming to the door is going to spoil our times together."

Any time a woman sees that her husband is willing to be this tender, kind, gentle lover she can put up with many things. A wife can accept small inconveniences like an occasional late dinner. She can cope with those emergency times when he is called away, and their plans are cancelled. She and the children can be far more tolerant of her husband's work because they know when he is home—he is theirs.

Not only can she put up with many things when she

knows her husband is a gentle lover, but her ability to respond sexually is greatly enhanced. Contrary to an old established opinion, women are not only romanticists, but are very capable of enjoying a fully rewarding sex life. This may come as a news bulletin to some of you because your wife has been sexually cool (to the point of frigid) for years. You have assumed she didn't like sex or she didn't seem to need it.

Most of us go into marriage with a suitcase full of misinformation, half-truths, and preconceived ideas; we are particularly susceptible to the sex knowledge we gleaned from our early years.

If your parents were born in the first twenty-five years of this century, you were probably reared with the idea that sex was the biggest no-no of your life. Many Christian parents viewed sex only for procreation; anything else was lumped under fornication or adultery. Your wife may have entered marriage after being reared by a mother who either ignored sex altogether, or carefully spelled out the three *D*'s of sex: Duty, Dull, and Dirty!

She may have had any number of sexual needs or feelings when you were first married. However, many women have heard since childhood, "nice girls don't talk about 'it' to anyone." Your wife can't even talk to you, her husband. The years of marriage roll on, and both of you are caught in the vise of your background and upbringing.

You, with your background, may have brought to marriage the masculine myth which theorizes you're a *real man* about sex if you are able to *conquer* your woman during intercourse.

Or, worse, you may have brought to your marriage bed the ridiculous and dishonest belief that men are wise beyond belief and know everything about sexuality. (What man in his right mind would admit he didn't know everything?) The first time (and any time after that) things go quietly wrong during intercourse a man has to keep up his pretense that he knows and understands everything that's

happened—even if he doesn't have the foggiest notion.
This type of dishonesty turns off the learning process of
loving, it cancels out any new discovery he might make,
and forces his sexual experiences to be very limited at
best.

Many women are mistakenly sure men invented sex,
patented it, and have kept it number one on today's priority list. However we all know it was not man, but God,
who thought up the whole idea of marriage and human
sexuality. It was God, watching Adam's restlessness in the
Garden of Eden, who mused, ". . . It isn't good for man
to be alone; I will make a companion for him, a helper
suited to his needs" (Genesis 2:18).

Adam never asked God to fix up a date with some foxy
chick. In fact the idea just never crossed his mind. It was
God who tapped Adam on the shoulder and said, "Boy, do
I have a surprise for you!" (Or words to that effect.) Ever
since that day, men have been throwing up their hands
and proclaiming loudly and clearly, "I'll never understand women!" And women have been sure most men are
sex maniacs.

My mother asked me the day after I was married,
"Well, was it terrible?" She wanted to know if Dick had
done this-and-such-and-such and I could hardly believe
her questions.

"No, Mother," I said. "Everything was just beautiful—
what makes you think it was otherwise?"

She quickly said, "Well, you know—most men are like
beasts. Your father isn't—he's sweet. But other men—
they're terrible." I never knew how she got her information about other men but I suspect she was merely enlarg-
ing on the thought patterns of her peer group.

Most of us forget that God designed male and female,
and they are extremely different from each other. I'm
sure, as a man, you've noticed your wife doesn't think, or
respond like you. Instead of letting this difference between you upset you and bog you down, let me offer you

some encouragement. God did not in any way, shape, or form make Adam and Eve alike. In fact, He created them entirely different! I'm not sure about all the reasons why He did that, but keeping everything extremely interesting might have been one of His motivating factors.

Bennard R. Wiese and Urban G. Steinmetz wrote about these differences and they included two diagrams which are most revealing.

In their informative book *Everything You Need to Know to Stay Married and Like It*, they pointed out that both a man and woman begin their relationship with mutual attraction. However, after attraction, the male moves into sex, and finally love. With the woman it's the reverse. She has to have love first in order to mature into sex. (That brings us right back to love-starts-in-the-kitchen.) As their book states:

What she desires most of all in marriage is love. This is what she wants from her children and from her husband. She wants and needs love. Sex she wants too, but for the female, sex is a by-product or self-fulfillment of love in the sense that she must first have love before she can reach a totally complete mature sexuality.

Get that concept under your hat, dear sir, and you'll see how very important it is to demonstrate and practice the gentle kindnesses I talked of in the preceding chapter. Women have been created differently, not only emotionally, but certainly biologically as well. Our sexual responses and drives operate on a different level from yours.

During foreplay a woman's arousal may be considerably slower than that of her husband. If I had one message to give to husbands today it would be: *Slow down.* The finely tuned lover learns to pace himself because it brings the most fulfilling results.

(For what it's worth, men—my message to women is: Concentrate and focus!) Your wife may be easily distracted, especially by the patter of little feet running toward the bedroom. She may have to overcome the years of brainwashing about not having sexual feelings or desires. Some women have suppressed those desires so long that it takes a great deal of focusing on these feelings to bring them to life again.

The message for you of *slow down* goes for all aspects of loving. Telling her you love her, showing her by acts of kindness in the kitchen, and taking time in loving foreplay and gentle caressing before intercourse are just some of the ways to become one flesh.

Many men do not know what really turns their wives on during lovemaking. They have never asked—and she has never said—so their sexual life becomes a "time to get it over with" and "the sooner the better."

A young couple with some real difficulties was talking to me one afternoon. One of the problems was sex. The wife had withheld sex from her husband for several months. We talked about their sex life earlier in their marriage; she assured me, even then, it was pretty bad and she hated it.

I asked her what her husband did during foreplay that really turned her into a tense and unwilling participant. Because she and her husband were desperate, she leveled with me and shared the details. After I listened a bit, I said, "Did you ever tell him to stop that, or do this, or try something else?"

"Oh, no, I couldn't do that. I never talked about sex with him," came the answer.

Her husband was sitting there listening to the conversation and his face was lined with a mass of question marks.

"Why didn't you tell me you didn't like what I was doing? I thought it was just fine—I had no idea that turned you off."

There, for all three of us to see, sat the unvarnished truth. Those two people had been married eight years, had communicated about everything under the sun from budgets to babies except for their feelings on sexual matters. Refusing to communicate those feelings had prevented them from truly becoming one flesh and knowing that special God-designed joy intercourse can bring.

We need to help each other by verbal and nonverbal (touching) communication to let our wants and preferences be known. Never shut the door on this kind of sharing because from time to time needs and desires change. We never reach the point where we *know all.* Because about then, what felt good last month doesn't feel good now, and so the channels of communication must be kept open. But the marvelous thing is—as you keep those lines open between you—no one will know better than you what really pleasures your wife and makes her respond to your loving.

It is not my intention, in this chapter, to give fuel to any anxiety in your heart about the caliber of your sexual performance. Rather, I'd like you to think about these God-given reasons for sex in your life to better understand male and female sexuality.

Some Christians have maintained that copulation was only for procreation. At the other end of the spectrum is the *Playboy* philosophy which says copulation is only for recreation. In truth, both (and not necessarily simultaneously) were created for joyous sexuality in our lives.

Meaningful intercourse in marriage, the kind which involves these purposes of sex, is made up of two words: *Giver* and *Receiver.* We need to develop the exchange of both roles. Sometimes you are the pure giver. Other times you're the pure receiver. There are even some times when you are both! Unfortunately in some marriages one partner is the giver or receiver all of the time. Consequently their sexual life is somewhat boring and lopsided. But if we love our partner with the "What can I do for you that will pleasure you?" concept firmly in our hearts and minds, we will alternate the giving and receiving roles during lovemaking.

You may have trouble just being the pure giver or the pure receiver, but try it. It can be a most rewarding, fantastic experience for you.

It has been rightly said that making love is an art, as it does take practice. Not the actual act of intercourse, anybody can manage that with little or no training, but real lovemaking is definitely an acquired art. The "becoming one flesh" is something we work at for years. Practicing lovemaking and the years which are needed to develop it are the best reasons why premarital and extramarital sex don't work too well.

A man I'll call George used to work at my husband's bank. George had recently been divorced and was now establishing himself as the most eligible bachelor about town. Each day the bank tellers excitedly gossiped about his latest word, and the male officers crowded around him at lunch to hear about his most recent sexual escapade. Months went by and George seemed to be living a hysterically marvelous, enviable life. He had taken up residence in a swinging-singles apartment at the beach and boasted about having sex every night (and twice on Sundays) with glorious girls. As one married banker marveled, "George really has it made."

But one afternoon George came up to my husband's desk and haltingly said, "Uh, Dick, could I talk to you about something?"

Then, as nearly as Dick can remember, this is what

George related. "You know, Dick, I've really got it made. I'm free from the attachments of marriage. I've got this great pad at the beach and I go to bed with one sexy gal after another. I come and go as I please and I do my own thing. But something is really bothering me and I can't figure it out. Every morning as I get dressed for work I look into the mirror and I think, 'What was last night's sexy little game all about? Sure the girl was good-looking. She was good in bed and she left this morning without bugging me, but is that all there is in life?' I asked myself, 'If this life-style is what every guy thinks he wants, why am I so depressed? Why do I feel a cold nothingness all the time?' "

He stopped, leaned closer to Dick, and quietly continued. "I know the guys here think it would be fantastic to have this kind of liberated freedom but honestly, Dick, I hate this life." He sat back and paused for a few seconds and then wistfully added, "You know what I'd really like? I'd like to go home tonight, smell dinner cooking, hug my wife hello, and spend the evening telling her and showing her how much I love her. I'd like to go to bed with her and not have to prove my virility, not have to sexually perform above the call of duty, but just give her love, and go to sleep knowing she'd be there in the morning."

Practicing the art of loving, even enjoying a welcome after hours of not seeing each other, and pleasuring each other for years—these were the ingredients missing from George's sexual life. Changing partners every night hardly left much time for continuity or development of growth and enjoyment. In fact instant, pleasurable sex did the opposite of what George (and many others) thought. The act of intercourse became just that—an empty, meaningless act, devoid of any real purpose.

I am convinced that the rise in infidelity in our country today is in part due to a myth—the myth that flaunts an uninhibited sex adventure once in a while as being a cure for everything. We are all brainwashed into thinking that if we could just get into George's position in life we'd have a ball. If we could let ourselves go, drop our puritanical beliefs and guilts, and give ourselves to swinging sexually with someone, we would receive these benefits: Our failures, our resentments, and our personal loneliness would go away. A man enters an affair in search of fulfillment, and a woman in search of a romantic dream. Both are disheartened by the end results. Gradually, both parties become sadly aware that their sexual intercourse has been just exactly that, an act of sexual intercourse, and absolutely nothing more. It is at that moment that the failures, resentments, and loneliness return to each of them just as big as they always were. The affair is over and all that's left is the guilt and desperate feelings of frustration.

Married love, giving love, and especially the tender love has much more to offer. It was Dr. Bernard Ramm, in his excellent book on Christian ethics, *The Right, the Good and the Happy,* who wrote about the emptiness of sex alone:

Happy sexuality has prepared the way for happy sex, and it doesn't work in reverse. There are certainly thousands of marriages every year that end up in the divorce court because the couple has the relationship of sex and sexuality in the reverse order.

Or to put it another way, sex must exist in the context of sexuality which means a significant relationship of the sexes before sexual intercourse; and it intends a meaningful relationship after intercourse. If intercourse is a mere event, a mere happening, it is bound to be superficial and frustrating. Sexuality presupposes a set of real relationships before intercourse and a life of mutuality after intercourse. In this context there is fulfillment in sex. But when there is sex with no sexuality then sex becomes episodic and superficial.

I drew my own diagrams when I read his words. Here is the sex act.

But it must be preceded by a meaningful relationship,

and followed by a maturing relationship.

If you take away both relationships you are left with the

and that is nothing but a bottomless well of aloneness.

Before I close this chapter on the gentle lover, I'd like to suggest an assignment. Of course you don't have to carry it out, and there is no way I am going to check up on you to see that you've done it, but for your own sake, I wish you'd try it.

It's quite simple, really. Take an ordinary sheet of paper and write at the top of it: "Five Things I Really Appreciate About You." Then number and list five things about your wife you sincerely appreciate. They do not have to be sensational, talented, gifted types of things, but they must be real attributes you honestly like. Do not make up things and flatter her, because she will immediately sense it and reject your list. Remember flattery is *unearned* praise. Appreciation means telling her about the delicious way she cooks chicken, or how diplomatic she was with the kids, or what you like about her hair or figure. But be truthful and honest.

Sometimes over the years we experience a lessening of wonderment about each other. We take our love for granted, and so years can go by without either of us expressing a loving thought. We see no need to reinforce our love by any written or verbal statements. We are so wrong—for we all need the gentle reassurance. Best we do it before the grave shuts off all avenues of opportunity.

Write your list—making it as brief or as long as you want, and give it to her when she is in the kitchen. Give it to her early in the evening, and not just before you go to bed. (She'll suspect your motives if it's too close to bedtime.) When she asks, "What's this for?" just tell her you're not too good and not too quick in letting her know how you feel, so you thought it was about time. Tell her you sincerely meant the list, and that you hope the list lets her know she is loved.

As I was giving this assignment to a group of men at a seminar, one raised his hand and questioned, "Is this list of five things really necessary? I mean, my wife knows I love her, and I'm not a very good letter (or note) writer. I don't know if doing something like this is worth it or not."

I said, "You do the assignment and then you tell me if it was worth it."

The next morning was Sunday and I was to be the speaker for this man's church service. Just as I entered the vestibule he rushed over to me and excitedly grabbed my arm.

"How'd it go?" I asked.

"Well," he began rather breathlessly, "first of all I found eight things, not five, that I really love about her, so I wrote them down and gave them to her before dinner last night."

"Then what happened?" I asked and I realized the man's face was becoming quite flushed and red. It was slightly awkward for me because I guessed his evening had been just wonderful, and their time together sexually had been unusually good.

"Spare me the details," I hurried on to say.

"Okay," he said, "but I've got to say one thing."

"All right—what?"

And then he said one word—*"Wow!"*

We both laughed and I went on up to the platform.

The choir came in. Just before the service started the man's wife leaned over from the soprano section and whispered, "My husband wrote me the first love letter in all our years of marriage. It was just marvelous. I begged him to tell me what you talked about with the men at yesterday's seminar but he wouldn't. Finally because I bugged him so much about it, he said, 'Honey, I'm never going to tell you what Joyce Landorf said to the men today —I'm just going to spend the rest of my life *showing you.*'"

The issue of being a gentle lover and the functions of sex in our lives is not nearly so important as the world around us makes it out to be. On the other hand, the "marriage bed" is definitely to be a part of our lives, our existence, and our enjoyment. The book of Hebrews tells us, "Let marriage be held in honor among all, and let the marriage bed be undefiled . . ." (13:4 RSV).

For those most intimate times of mingling and becoming one flesh, I would pray God's wisdom and direction. Since He created your human sexuality you can trust Him, even with your love life, to make your marriage bed a bed of joy and gentle loving.

SCRIPTURES

Love	1 Corinthians 13:4–8
	1 John 4:8–10, 16–19
	John 15:12
	2 Peter 1:6–8
Rights of loving	1 Corinthians 7:3–5
	1 Corinthians 11:3
Sex within marriage	Genesis 2:23, 24
	1 Corinthians 11:11
	Proverbs 5:18, 19
	Ephesians 5:31
Sex outside marriage	1 Corinthians 6:15–20
	Proverbs 4:23–26
Experiencing God's love	Ephesians 3:17–19

RECOMMENDED READING

La Haye, Tim and Beverly. *The Act of Marriage*. Grand Rapids: Zondervan Publishing House, 1976.

Wheat, Dr. Ed and Gaye. *Intended for Pleasure*. London: Scripture Union 1979.

Wiese, Bennard, and Steinmetz, Urban. *Everything You Need to Know to Stay Married and Like It*. Grand Rapids: Zondervan Publishing House, 1975.

8

A Most Unlikely Man

> Never envy the wicked! Soon they fade away like grass
> and disappear. Trust in the Lord instead. Be kind and
> good to others; then you will live safely here in the land
> and prosper, feeding in safety. Be delighted with the
> Lord. Then he will give you all your heart's desires.
>
> PSALMS 37:1–4

This Scripture is at first deceptively simple, but if you
investigate it to any degree, you find it's rather a tall
order. When it says to not envy the wicked and just trust
the Lord you think, "Ah, that's not so hard."

Then you remember the conniving little backstabber at
the office who got the promotion in spite of your qualifica-
tions and seniority. Picturing him as fading "away like
grass" doesn't help either, and trusting the Lord makes
very little sense at the moment. Being kind to others and
prospering, delighting yourself in the Lord, and receiving
your heart's desires reads well in the Bible on Sunday. But
in the chilly light of Monday morning, the words bog
down in your mind as impractical and rather unrealistic.

Is God serious when He lays down the rules and conditions of life, and does He really mean to give your heart's
desires in return for obedience? In fact, does He know
exactly what your heart actually desires? The answer is
definitely and absolutely yes. Unequivocally, yes!

One of my publishers, Bob Hawkins, said once, "You
know, Joyce, as I was driving my car to the office I
thought, 'It's so easy to trust the Lord when everything is
going along very smoothly. But it's so hard when all things
seem to be wrong.' " Right on! Trusting God with your
life, your wife, your family, and your work is a very scary

thing, especially if everything looks as if it's flying apart. It's like driving at night through a long tunnel and having all your lights short-out. The car keeps moving, but in the darkness you become disoriented and lose all sense of direction.

For years, at our former church, our dear friend Dr. Keith Korstjens was our Sunday-school teacher. I remember one morning, when four words out of his lesson really caught me. I went around and around with those words as if we were riding some mental Ferris wheel together. Keith gave several illustrations of God taking a most unlikely man and making him into more of a man than he had ever been before. His words "a most unlikely man" were the ones that clung to my thoughts. They have not left me yet. I'm still going over them as they ride around in my mind.

Isn't this what God does for each one of us? Aren't we each a most unlikely man or woman until we let go and really let God take over? If our world was taking a vote on us, wouldn't we all qualify for "The Most Unlikely to Succeed" title? Some of us would have to readily agree we are highly unlikely candidates for being the person God wants us to be. Living our daily lives in cheerful obedience to God's laws, specifications, and principles sometimes completely overwhelms us. The task of being God's man seems placed too high for us to reach, too misty and vague to catch, and too expensive for our budget.

What about you? Perhaps you decided obedience to God is too high a price; if asked you would describe yourself as a self-made man, independent of God, and indifferent to His plans. (I don't really believe for one second this is a man truly 100 percent self-made.) I've known good men, men of character and principles, who were without God. However, being without God they had to become self-sufficient and rather egocentric. Self, by necessity, had to be the center of their existence. While they did not misuse or abuse their ego, living without God did have

one serious drawback. It left them with no higher authority and no greater power to fall back on—if and when
their natural resources ran out.

I have seen the marriages of these men succeed without
God for years. The couple seemed to be utterly complete
in each other and quite self-sufficient. They needed nothing from anybody. Then the husband or the wife has surgery and cancer is discovered; or a child of theirs dies one
unforeseen day; or the business, once so sound, breaks
apart like a fragile glass, shattering them into bankruptcy;
then their marriage splinters and snaps under the strain.
This couple may or may not turn to God during the crisis,
they may or may not survive as individuals, but one thing
is sure—they are never the same again. Without God during their crisis, they are seriously handicapped.

On the other hand, thousands of Christian people who
have given God their lives have said the identical thing
after life has struck a tragic blow, "I don't know what we
would have done without the Lord." God longs to take
you—no matter how much *a most unlikely man* you
think you are—and make you into so much more.

Consider what God has done in the past with these
unlikely men:

An old, sterile man named Abraham became the father
of all the nations.

A boy sold as a slave by his very own brothers became
Joseph, governor of Egypt.

A stuttering Moses became God's chosen spokesman for
the Hebrew nation.

An adulterer and murderer, forgiven by God, became
David, king of Israel.

A religious bigot and chief persecutor of Christians
named Saul became Paul, one of our beloved theology
teachers.

A blundering, outspoken fisherman named Peter became God's chosen leader.

A despised tax collector named Matthew, along with

other ordinary men, became the pens which gave us God's Holy Scriptures.

I could go on, but I'm sure you are ahead of me. God can do anything with you if you'll let Him. He will not stomp all over your life. He will not break down the door of your heart and order you to submission. No. Rather, He waits, knocks, and waits some more, until you open your life's door to Him.

When I think of things God has done and is continuing to do in the life of my husband, I can see that growth is a two-way street. God teaches, Dick learns; God rules, Dick obeys; God blesses, and Dick receives. There seems to be a never-ending process between them. God never stops and Dick never arrives—they both just continue to continue.

As I've watched this I've seen several thought processes which are necessary if growth is to take place. The first process to consider, if you—a most unlikely man—are to be the man God intends, goes like this:

1. *You may need a realignment of attitudes.* After you have asked God for His forgiveness in your own life, then you have to take a long, hard look at Ephesians 4:32 in regard to forgiving others.

A tough and tender man is a man who daily practices genuine and complete acceptance of his wife and family. He gives them the right to be what they are and he accepts the whys and wherefores of how they feel. Realigning your thoughts in this direction will be impossible if you have not preceded acceptance with forgiveness.

I had to forgive Dick for his master's degree in neatness and orderliness, and for his narrow-minded way of doing some things. Just hours after our wedding I found out my husband was human (a small fact I didn't necessarily want to acknowledge because it might mean he had flaws or was imperfect some way). I certainly didn't want to forgive him for being a neat toothpaste-tube roller. To me it makes more sense to squeeze it in the middle. (It's faster, too.) So it took me years to forgive and accept Dick's neatness, and then only because we had become Christians. Daily, even now, I see Dick's forgiveness toward me being practiced. He has to do it daily because each morning and night I leave my clothes lying around.

Together we have had the experience of forgiving and accepting our children's actions or rebellions. There have been hundreds of things in our daily lives we have forgiven and accepted. Some have been good things, good traits, or even talents. Others have been bad habits, annoying idiosyncrasies or little quirks in our personalities; but forgiveness and acceptance is essential for relationships to grow.

After I'd locked the back door and then watched Dick as he checked it, I heard the Lord say clearly, "Joyce, he's checking the back door to see if it really is locked because that's the way I've made him. I have made him a precise, decisive detail-man. That's why he's good at banking. Now, you forgive him for being neat and orderly and accept him as *I* have made him!" I never thought of forgiving a man because he checks up on me or is neat, but that's exactly what happened. Dick has forgiven and accepted my messiness. While it's true that during our twenty-some years of marriage I have become a little neater and Dick has become a little less tense over procedure, we still have had to forgive each other.

A man or woman is never taller and never stands straighter than when he or she will forgive others and is willing to ask forgiveness of others. The prideful act of forgiving others for their trespasses against us but not being willing to ask forgiveness of them, is the height of hypocrisy. One word about apologies. Someone once said, "An apology should honestly mean, I'm sorry I did that and I sincerely intend to never do it again."

Your wife may have some things in her life which you have never thought of forgiving and accepting. She may be overweight, when you adore slimness. She may be a brunette, when blondes are more your speed. She may be very smart, with a college degree, while you never finished high school. How have you handled these looks, abilities, talents, or flaws in her life? If you've nagged at her to change, you've probably not succeeded too well. However, if you've really forgiven her for being the way she is, for looking the way she does, and for acting the way she does, you're on your way to creating a healthy emotional climate at your house. Incidentally, sometimes merely forgiving your partner for something is enough for that person to want to change. It's funny how that works.

There are some things you cannot change, and that becomes step one in forgiveness. Change what you can change, but forget the impossible. (Maybe she's tried 101 diets and has gained weight with each one. At least she tried.)

Step two in forgiving comes with realizing that wherever two people live and exist, they will have differences. In our house there is only one way to do everything, and that's Dick's way. As soon as I forgave and accepted the policy, the in-fighting slowed down considerably. For instance, I know better than to pack our picnic basket or a box of books when we are moving because, as sure as I do it, I've done it wrong. (My husband suffers from a correct-packing-procedure disease he picked up years ago when he was a box boy in a grocery store.) Over the years I've learned that Dick's way is (about 95 percent of the time) the right way. So I've stopped fighting it and acceptance has become possible. (It's really horrible to live with someone who is right nine times out of ten—in fact it's sickening!)

Living within the attitude of forgiveness requires daily attention. It costs to forgive and it also hurts sometimes, but forgiveness is the key to acceptance. Our daughter Laurie wrote us a letter on our wedding anniversary a few years back; I've included it here because you'll be able to see the impact our forgiveness to each other has made in her life.

Dear Mom and Dad,

So many times lately at work [she's a waitress] I have told people that the two of you wanted to go a week early on your vacation so you could be alone.

Most people just looked up at me and gave me a little smile that said, "Ya, sure. Tell me about it."

I just looked back at them and explained, "They're still so much in love. They have a very special marriage."

Their little smile returned and I knew that probably they didn't believe me.

It makes me sad inside to see these people come into the restaurant with so little to say to each other. Then people like you and Dad come in—with so much to say. (Even if you've been with each other all day!)

Mom and Dad, your marriage has taught me so much. One of the things I've learned is the importance of believing and trusting in each other.

If and when I get married I want my marriage to be my own, but I want it to be built with the special kind of bricks that you have used; the bricks of communication, love, patience, understanding, and above all, the brick of forgiveness.

I thank you and the Lord, too, that you both decided to make things in your marriage work. It was years ago that you made the decision—but it was the best thing you probably ever did in your lifetime.

I love you both so much—have a very special anniversary.

With all my love,
LAURIE

The "brick of forgiveness" she said, and rightly so. Building a man or a marriage takes those special bricks.

If God is to take you, a most unlikely man, and develop your whole being, you may have to realign your attitudes on forgiveness and you may need this second step.

2. *You may need to change.* Even anticipating change is scary. For instance, a woman fears having to move her household again. A man is apprehensive about losing his job. Couples who have never prepared financially for their later years fear the changes they may experience when retirement comes. All of us fear the unknown, but one of the biggest threats to our security is the possibility of things changing. Our stomach knots up within us—as if we were about to come down an uncharted river full of rushing rapids, swirling waters, and unexpected rocks— whenever we anticipate change. Yet being unwilling to change may, in the end, destroy you, taking with it all you really love.

I remember a woman telling me about her daughter's divorce. The daughter was married to a fine young man for four years; in the first year of their marriage he had become a policeman. In the months and years to follow, police work had consumed all of the husband's time, thoughts, energies, and involvement. They separated and came back together again several times. The husband was hooked on law enforcement as if it were an addictive drug, and eventually it blotted his wife out of existence.

The mother said, "The last straw was broken when my daughter had lumps removed from both breasts and her husband would not take off from work to be with her or visit her at the hospital." Then sadly she added, "It's strange, but after the divorce was final, then he wanted to change. But, of course, by then it was too late." Refusing to change, stubbornly, egotistically demanding your right to stand pat, may cost you everything you now hold dear.

Earlier in this book I said we are not changed by an outside force—like a nagging, critical wife. Real and lasting change comes from within! It comes because *we want to change.* It must be an inner, not an outer-directed motivation.

To be aware of the need to change and then postpone it or procrastinate about it may be disastrous. Change can begin now, this minute, and it may come just in the nick of time for your marriage. A marriage counselor of considerable experience said, "If either or both the husband and the wife are not willing to try to change the patterns of their lives, and I cannot scare, threaten or force them to try change, I end the session. I open my desk drawer and fish out the first divorce lawyer's card I come to and hand it to them. They leave me no choice."

It was C. S. Lewis in his book *God in the Dock* who said, "Of all the awkward people in your house or job there is only one whom you can improve very much." He was talking straight to you and to me. Somehow, we always push change off on someone else's shoulders. We hear a good sermon and we say, "I wish old Sam could have heard that. Now, there's a guy who really needed it." During a marital row between a couple, we hear one of them plead to the other, "We need counseling, please let's get some help with this problem." And the partner retorts, "You go—you're the one who needs help—I don't have any problem." We are quick to point out someone else's need for change and very slow to admit it in regard to ourselves. Of course, by projecting the blame on your mate and implying by a hundred different methods that your mate should be the one to change her ways, you really end up playing an emotional blackmail game. If you say you are right and refuse to admit your part of the hassle, your marital strife will probably never even out. Both of you contribute to the problems of living together. I'm just glad that I can truthfully write—both of you can contribute to the solution, too!

If you do desire to change and you are willing to move into new areas, no matter how apprehensive you might feel, here are a few ideas to help you arrive at some new frontiers.

a) Learn to live with your past mistakes. We all make 'em! We all have 'em! The trick comes in learning from them what is to be learned, and then burying them.

There is a delightful story of a newlywed husband who was carpeting a room in his home. It was his first do-it-yourself project and he was very pleased with his results except for one slight imperfection. Down in one corner of the room there was a small bump under the rug. Since he didn't want his wife to see the problem, he walked over, stomped down, and finally managed to flatten the bump quite nicely. He was very pleased because then the whole carpet laid just right.

Much later that evening he had a terrible thought and said to his wife, "Have you seen my glasses and glasses case?"

She quickly responded, "Oh, sure, Hon, they are right here on the hall table. But I've been meaning to ask you all day—have you seen our parakeet?"

I'm sure it would take some time to live with that mistake, but I'm ready to bet he would be very willing to learn. We need to use a mistake for what it is, and we need to admit we can make mistakes. We should include in our vocabulary sentences like, "I'm sorry, I blew it! Now I'll try to correct my mistake."

In regard to change in general at your house, here is a second thought.

b) Let each partner move on his own path and at his own rate of speed toward change. Growth-producing change can come blindingly fast. I've seen it happen and it is possible.

I remember a woman who told me of her son's fantastic conversion to Christ. She described it like this, "He walked out of our house one night—a doper, a dropout, and an emotionally sullen boy. He went to a meeting with a new friend and met Christ. When he came home that

night, he woke us up to tell us his exciting good news. He
was radiant beyond words, he was ready to go back to
school and he asked us to forgive him for the hell he had
put us through. It was as if God Himself had pulled a
switch and within a few hours had turned him on to life.
The change was (and is) incredible!"

Change can be just like that, almost overnight, and
even spontaneous for some. Change can also be as slow as
the leaves which take all of September, October, and November to dress themselves in their red and golden hues
of autumn. Pace yourself and your mate accordingly, and
don't rush change. Give change a chance. I have one last
thought on change.

c) Consider how you (not your wife or children) could
change to make your life and marriage more meaningful.

I took a class one summer from the famous Dr. William
Glasser, M.D. and author. One of the statements he made
concerning change was very important. He said, "If a
couple is not willing to make changes, then there is little
hope for their marriage. The problem comes because people only change if they are willing and someone has got
to make the first move."

I think the key questions here should be: Could you
contribute anything to make this marriage of yours better? and, Are you willing to make the first move? If you
can do something, do it. Make a plan or set some goals, but
get started, don't let your pride stop you or slow you
down.

My own husband's change has been extremely gradual.
I had very big ideas of changing him before we were
married, and then after marriage I really tried. But nothing worked. It was after we became Christians that I
began to see the first changes occur. Dick's stubbornness
went into a good kind of toughness, and his sensitivity to
me began a slow but warm development. Even in the last
five years I've seen new and different changes. I'm awe-

struck with gratitude to our Lord as the changes have
come because Dick was willing. He did it on his own. (I
do admit to a few times when he received an impatient
push from me, but on the whole I've been curbing my
impulse to shove.)

Several years ago I had my own radio program and one
of the secretaries who helped me was a wonderful gal
named Ginger Luber. Just a few weeks ago she wrote me
a letter which included a part about her husband, Gene.

It seems that often lately the Lord has reminded me of special
ways friends have guided me in the past. I have been trying to
contact these as they come to mind and to tell them "thank
you."

I am reminded of a time following a recording session at
KBBI—you shared with me the fact that God hadn't given
Gene to me to change him, but to love him.

I can't count the times I've rehearsed that to myself in the
years since as I have caught myself trying to change him.

And so for that counsel and many other helpful words and
kindness, I just want to say thank you.

She learned early that she could not change Gene and
theirs has been a creative, working marriage.

Only you can change. Ask the sovereign King of all
kings for help; He is ready to assist you in feeling, seeing,
and experiencing change without fear or panic. To
change may mean to break old habits and reestablish new
ones, but God can (and does) give you the patience in that
area also.

After forgiveness and change, the last quality you may
need if God is to work in depth in your life is this one.

3. *You may need to make a commitment to effort.* It was
about five years after our conversion to Christ when our
pastor preached a stirring message to men on their commitment to effort. Near the close of his message he asked

the men of our congregation to either begin a relationship
with God or renew their commitment. Then he invited
only the men of the audience to come to the front of the
church for prayer. He called for those men to come who
were *ready to become God's men.* He used one of his
favorite expressions when he said, "I want men to paint
or get off the ladder."

In a matter of minutes, from every aisle in the church,
came hundreds of men. What thrilled me most was the
sight of my husband. He was one of the first to leave his
seat and stand before our pastor.

As I said, we had become Christians five years earlier,
so on the way home I questioned, "What were your reasons for going forward this morning?"

He answered, "I needed to make a public commitment
to God, to you, to my family, and before my friends because *I am going to be His man."*

Without sounding corny or maudlin, I can honestly say
Dick turned a new corner that day. It was almost as if God
truly honored Dick's commitment. I watched as God
began to mold, shape, and direct this God-aimed man and
the years have rolled up some pretty graphic facts. God's
direction, since Dick's commitment, has extended to
every facet of Dick's life and personality. His wife, his
family, his work, and even his pleasure hours have evi-
denced God's planning and blessing.

The steps of a righteous man, we are told in Psalm 37,
are ordered of God. The Living Bible puts it well when
it says, "The steps of good men are directed by the Lord.
He delights in each step they take. If they fall it isn't fatal,
for the Lord holds them with his hand" (v. 23, 24). I firmly
believe God begins to order and direct the steps of a
righteous man the moment God sees the man take his first
step toward commitment.

The awesome, incredible responsibility of being a husband and father is not possible without God's magnificent
grace and man's determined effort. Would you like your

wife to be that lovely, energetic, strong woman we read of in Proverbs 31? She's going to need several things to bring that into reality: a vigorous, healthy faith in Christ; a self-disciplined effort to her commitments; and a husband who will be a partner to such an adventure.

Just knowing what's right, or just being well-read on marriage and life in general, is not enough. The effort to act on our information is absolutely necessary if God is to turn any of us "unlikely people" into men and women *extraordinaire*.

C. S. Lewis in *Mere Christianity* wrote, "The Son of God became a man to enable men to become sons of God." Becoming real sons of God will not be possible without your saying, *"I will* be a son of God." David said it over and over in Psalms and I'm convinced he said it many days when everything was wrong and his world looked like it had just spun out of control. Yet he said,

I *will* praise Thee,
I *will* bless the Lord,
I *will* be joyful,
I *will* sing,
I *will* trust,
I *will* obey,

and many more. His commitment to effort seemed inexhaustible. Since what I am suggesting in this last chapter is very difficult, and requires patient, plodding, consistent effort, you may ask if it really is all worth it.

I've already told you about my husband's decision to really be God's man. That happened a number of years ago, and we have all been amazed at God's leading ever since. One Father's Day, before we moved from the Pomona area of Los Angeles to our present home, Dick was asked, as a layman in our church, to give a brief testimony in the morning service about his life in Christ. As he spoke I couldn't help but remember the morning so long ago when he made his commitment to effort. Dick had truly sought to obey God's instructions and God, in return, had given Dick some of the deepest (even hidden) desires of his heart. The sermon which followed Dick's brief talk was one of Dr. Ted Cole's finest, and as he closed, he called for men to respond to the call of God. Once more our church watched with eyes brimming with tears as many men instantly came forward.

Our daughter was in the audience and she came home to write this letter to her father. As you read it ask yourself whether a commitment to effort is worth the trouble or not.

My precious Dad,

What words could one use to express the feelings I had inside me as I watched and listened to you speak this morning?

"Pride and joy" cannot even begin to express what I felt down inside.

Oh, Dad, you touched my heart so deeply. I cannot imagine what you (and Dr. Ted) did for the hearts of the men who came forward. They knew, as well as the rest of the congregation, that what you said was not only true but said from the bottom of your heart.

Dad, as you spoke you renewed inside of me the ability to "wait" for just the right husband. I'll wait five years (or more) for him if he will be as special and dear as you.

Everything Dr. Ted said this morning so fitted you as a father and husband. Mom cannot help but fall more in love with you as each day fades into another. In the same way that her responding affects you, it also reflects upon Rick, Teresa and me. We not only feel it but we are warmed by the love that you share.

My heart was filled with joy as each father came forward this morning. Probably because I so hoped that maybe now their children will know the joy of having a father who has chosen to be God's man.

I love you, Daddy, you'll always hold a special place in my heart.

When the day comes that you go to be with Jesus, my heart will still be filled with happiness. My mind will think (and smile) about all the things we did together—as a family and then as a father and daughter.

Thank you Dad for all the things that you have given to me. As Mom would say, "I'm the Richest Lady in Town," and that I am!

All my love,

LAURIE

There it is—a difficult decision made years ago, but worth every ounce of effort it required.

In *Mere Christianity* C. S. Lewis wrote eloquently,

The more we let Christ take us over, the more truly ourselves we become. Christ invented all the different men that we millions were intended to be. It is as if our real selves are all waiting for us in Him. The more we resist Him, the more we are dominated by our heredity, upbringing, surroundings, and natural desires. What we call "my wishes" are greatly determined by diet, propaganda, other people's opinions, or even the suggestion of devils. We are not, in the natural state, nearly so much persons as we like to think; most of what each one calls "me" can be explained by looking at outside influences. When we give ourselves up to Christ's personality, we start to have real distinct personalities of our own.

I think I speak for Christian women all over the world when I say we do not expect a man to be something he is not—some spiritual giant of the faith, a romantic knight in shining armor, or a man of unlimited wealth, power, and influence. No, these are not the qualities we long for. We want a man to be himself. God has designed each of us to be highly original with many varied skills and talents. We want our man to be uncompromisingly tough of character and gently tender of heart.

A poem, entitled "Introspection," by a husband and father named Herbert Parker, spoke to my heart, not long ago, and moved me deeply. Read these lines and feel the sensitivity of this tough yet tender man of God.

Introspection

To get his goodnight kiss he stood
  Beside my chair one night
And raised an eager face to me,
  A face with love alight.

And as I gathered in my arms
  The son God gave to me,
I thanked the boy for being good,
  And said I hoped he'd always be.

His little arms crept round my neck.
  And then I heard him say,
Four simple words I'll never forget,
  Four words that made me pray.

They turned a mirror on my soul
  On secrets no one knew.
They startled me—but I hear them yet,
  For he said, "I'll be like you."

I sense this man is like all of us—a little overwhelmed by the task of being God's person in the changing world of today. Unlikely man? Yes—but isn't that whom God uses best?

So, above all, be God's man, no matter *how* unlikely you may feel. As the man of today you will not have an easy task in becoming the tough and tender man I have described. However, if you have truly laid your life and loves in God's hands, you have won half the battle.

Press on, Dear Man. All our days here are so brief, but the time spent in learning to be God's man is worth every second of it!

SCRIPTURES

Forgiving each other	Matthew 18:21, 22
	Colossians 3:13
	Ephesians 4:32
Loving	1 John 3:18
	2 John 1:6

Change	Psalms 101:2
	Psalms 37:34
	James 1:5, 6
Commitment	Matthew 21:22
	Colossians 3:10, 11
	Mark 9:23
	Psalms 37:23, 24
	Proverbs 20:24
	2 Timothy 3:1
	1 Timothy 6:11, 12

RECOMMENDED READING

Dobson, Dr. James. *Hide or Seek*. London: Hodder & Stoughton 1982.

Dobson, Dr. James. *Man to Man About Women*. Eastbourne: Kingsway Publications 1976.

Thatcher, Floyd and Harriett. *Long Term Marriage*. London: Hodder & Stoughton 1982.

How do you say 'I Love You'?
Expressing Love in Marriage

---

by Judson Swihart

Many husbands and wives love each other, but have difficulty in communicating that love. They seem to speak different languages. Each one says 'I love you' and hears 'I love you' in a different way.

The author shows how we can use the many languages of love in ways that are meaningful to both partners. He gives practical, down-to-earth suggestions to help us share the love of God as a reality in our homes.

This book has been a great help to us as a couple . . . There will be few who will not have something to learn from it, and we commend it with confidence and gratitude.

From the Foreword by
Canon Michael Green and his wife Rosemary

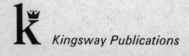

Kingsway Publications

Man to Man about Women

by James Dobson

It's time to be honest about ourselves. Today's society is involved in a pathetic search for personal pleasure.

Women's Lib is not so much a movement as a cry from the heart to be understood—as a God-given human being. Dr James Dobson attempts to set the matter right. He's a psychologist, husband and father. His writings are not theoretical but born of practical involvement in the problems confronted by women.

This book is for men and women—written by a man for men, but its aim is to understand one of God's greatest gifts to man—a woman!

Some of this book's topics—
    What causes depression in women
    The effect of fatigue and time pressure
    Sex machine or sex partner
    Menstrual and physiological problems
and a host of other down-to-earth factors.

Kingsway Publications

Strike the Original Match

by Charles Swindoll

To love and to cherish
For better, for worse
Till death us do part

The promises made when two people are married speak of love, commitment and permanence. But unless God's plan is followed, there is no foundation for the future.

Charles Swindoll believes God has given us the blueprint for marriages not only to last but to be enjoyed. There may be problems and issues to work through, but biblical principles are always realistic: they start with us where we are and redirect us step by step to God's original pattern.

'Few authors write with the insight and gift of communication enjoyed by Chuck Swindoll. His books are a beautiful blend of scriptural wisdom and practical advice for today. To read them is almost like having a conversation with a good friend who understands how families function best.'

JAMES DOBSON

Charles Swindoll lives in California with his wife and four children. He is widely respected for his pastoral and teaching ministry.

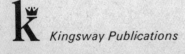

Kingsway Publications